Mr and Mrs Dutt

Mr and Mrs Dutt

Memories of our Parents

Namrata Dutt Kumar

Priya Dutt

Lustre Press
Roli Books

For Saachi, Trishala, Siya, Siddharth and
Priya's new baby on the way...
may the past light the future.

Foreword

People often think the children of film stars lead glamorous and exciting lives, attending countless parties and premieres, but as the children of Nargis and Sunil Dutt, we had a simple, down-to-earth life rooted in strong family values. We weren't brought up to think of our parents as famous actors, or even celebrities, nor were we raised as thoughtless and spoilt kids. To us Nargis and Sunil Dutt were just Mom and Dad – caring, warm and wonderful parents, as well as being a husband and wife deeply in love with one another.

The glitz of cinema wasn't an environment we knew and despite the fact that Mom had begun her career in the 1940s, we didn't see her movies until we were much older. Neither were Dad's film activities part of our lives. Of course once Sanjay started acting in 1980 (debuting in *Rocky*), we became more aware of the film world.

Although our parents came from amazingly different worlds, we had the benefit and joy of receiving the best two most unusual people could offer. After Mom's death in 1981, Dad took on both roles, becoming Mom and Dad to us. It was a magnificent transformation and another proof of how much they had loved each other.

Mom was given two names when she was born. Her Muslim mother called her Fatima Abdul Rashid, while her Hindu father named her Tejeshwari Uttamchand Mohanchand. But the world knew her as Nargis. When Dad was born, he was named Balraj Raghunath Dutt and later became

Top: Dad was always affectionate with us kids and never shied away from showing us his love.
Bottom: Mom applies *kajal* to Namrata, born on 5 January 1962.
Facing page: Mom often wore a ribbon in her hair when she was young. It is unclear whether Mom and Dad are pulling off or trying to put on little Sanjay's pants.
Preceding page 10: Mom and Sanjay pictured in our Bandra bungalow. Being the first born Sanjay was deeply attached to Mom.

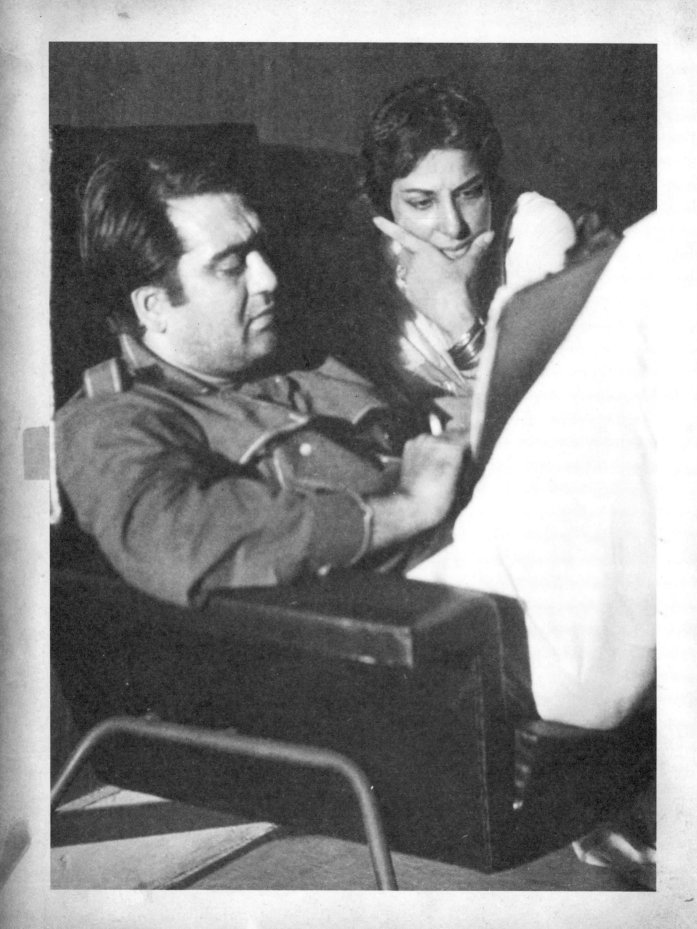

Above: Dad with Sanjay and Priya. There was always a strong bond between us siblings.
Facing page: Mom was closely associated with *Yaadein*, in which a sole character drives the narrative. Once Mom had taken us away on holiday, and Dad found himself in an empty house. His fear of loneliness runs through the film.

known as Sunil Dutt. The most incredible part of their story is how two such dissimilar individuals — a Hindu from rural Punjab and a sophisticated Bombayite born into a Muslim family — met and fell in love. The answer lies in the fact that if our parents were unconventional, our grandparents were even more so.

If the reader is looking for an understanding of the films Mom and Dad were involved with, or an analysis of their politics, this isn't the book to provide that view. *Mr and Mrs Dutt* is about their personal and very private lives, seen through precious memories of them. The reminiscences of us three children are at the heart of this book, which also includes letters and pages from childhood albums carefully preserved by our parents so that one day we might recall the invaluable days spent together. Countless photographs, old and worn files, tattered bits of papers and frayed scrap books help us to paint the story of our parents — where they came from, what they had meant to each other and what they continue to mean to us. The aim of this book is to share the things that Mom and Dad

Top: Celebrating Namrata's birthday as Sanjay lights the candle, toddler Priya looks on.
Bottom: Sanjay was born in 1959, two years after the considerable impact of *Mother India*, but Mom never regretted leaving a life of glamour and fame to raise her adored son.
Facing page: Dad with Sanjay and Priya. From an early age, we kids doted on Dad.

told us and taught us. And although the memories of our parents are not confined in this book to one point of view, it is Namrata who carries the narrative in the first person.

We are deeply grateful to our family and many friends who were so generous in recounting their memories of the past. We would like to thank Mr Dheeraj Chawda, Dayanita Singh, Shaukat Khan, Zahida Sahay, Jaywant Ulhal and Anil Gaba for contributing some rare photographs. Thank you to Kishwar and Meghnad Desai for their help. We would also like to thank our editor Nasreen Munni Kabir for her careful work on this book. There are thousands of people in many different countries who knew both Mom and Dad, and we continue to be deeply touched by their affection.

Mr and Mrs Dutt is a celebration and tribute to the exceptional people whom we knew as Mom and Dad. To friends and admirers, they will always be the most remarkable and special people. Seen from the eyes of their children, an objective and impartial view is perhaps an unrealistic expectation. In all humility and quite simply, this book is a sentimental journey through cherished memories.

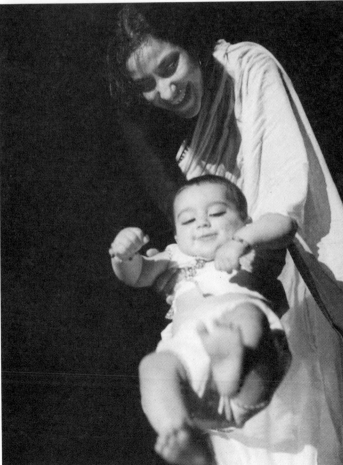

Namrata Dutt Kana   *Priya Dutt*

Mumbai, September 2007

The Beginning

Above: Jaddanbai surrounded by her grandchildren. Jaddanbai was India's first woman film and music director. She was also a famous *thumri* singer and noted disciple of Moijuddin Khan.
Left: In 1934, our grandparents settled in Bombay and Grandma made many friends in the film world. Jaddanbai's home was famously open to one and all.
Facing page: Our maternal grandfather, Mohan Babu (*standing on the right*), his brother (*standing, left*), our great-grandfather (*centre*) and his uncles are seated on either side of him.
Preceding page 18-19: It is said that Mom and Dad first met fleetingly at Bimal Roy's *Do Beegha Zameen* premiere in 1953. Dad was covering the premiere for a radio show and briefly interviewed Mom.

Our parents were born in opposite parts of pre-Partition India. Fatima was born on 1 June 1929 in Calcutta. She was the daughter of Uttamchand Mohanchand who belonged to a wealthy Rawalpindi family, and the famous and talented *thumri* singer Jaddanbai, who came from Chilbilla, a small village in Uttar Pradesh. Mohan Babu was studying to be a doctor and was supposed to go to London when he became entranced by Jaddanbai. It is said he heard her singing, perhaps in Calcutta or Lucknow, and fell instantly in love. In order to

marry her, he became a Muslim and took the name Abdul Rashid. However, throughout his life, he was called Mohan Babu. He was converted to Islam by the famous freedom fighter Maulana Abdul Kalam Azad. Mohan Babu paid a high price for his love as he had chosen to marry Jaddanbai despite the outrage and protests of his family. Subsequently, he was disowned and disinherited by them. He was a Mohyal Brahmin and, ironically, when Mom married Dad, she also married a Mohyal Brahmin. So life had come a full circle in a span of just 30 years. This is an extraordinary coincidence because the Mohyals are a small sect, who were said to have fought alongside the family of Prophet Mohammed in the war of Karbala, way back in the 7th century, when they were also called "Hussaini Brahmins."

Mohan Babu and Jaddanbai had a colourful and adventurous life full of song, music and cinema, moving from Calcutta to Lahore, and then finally settling down in Bombay on the coast of the Arabian Sea in 1934, when Mom was five years old. Here, Grandmother set up a production house and soon became the first woman in India to be a producer, scriptwriter, music composer, actor and singer. In no time an entourage of relatives and aspiring filmstars mushroomed around her and she became

Top (left): Mom's first film was the family drama *Talaash-e-Haq* (1935, C.M. Lohar). Grandmother composed the film's music and acted in it too. In those days, Mom was called "Baby Rani" and throughout her life, friends continued to call her "Baby."

Top (right): Mom was a true sport and here she is saving a school play from oblivion.

Bottom (left): She loved playing pranks. Here she is poised to spray colour on a friend during Holi.

Bottom (right): Mom celebrating Holi with Shammi Rabadi and Neelam, who were her contemporaries. Mom and Shammi aunty were inseperable and throughout her life, she counted amongst Mom's closest friends.

Top: Mom was known as "Pappo" to her nieces and nephews (*l to r*) Shahida, (Mom), Zahida, Rehana, Kookoo and Sadhana, Jaffar and (*right*) Sarwar.

Above: Affectionately called "Babuji," Mohan Babu's life was entirely changed when he fell in love with Jaddanbai.

Left: Jaddanbai, the famous Yakub with his familiar hat and Akhtar uncle (Jaddanbai's eldest son). Everyone in the film world called Grandma "Bibiji."

a huge film personality in Bombay during the 30s and 40s. Despite Jaddanbai's wealth and fame, Fatima was brought up in the Islamic faith, growing up in a close-knit family atmosphere along with her two older brothers, Akhtar and Anwar Hussain. Young Fatima was known to all as Baby, though the name on the door to the family's home read Fatima Abdul Rashid.

Family bonds were equally important for young Balraj. He was born in Khurd, a small village in the Jhelum District on 6 June 1929, only five days after Fatima's birth. Balraj grew up in the rough and tumble of rural life. He was the son of landlord and farmer Dewan Raghunath Dutt. His father died when Balraj was young and his courageous mother, Kulwanti Devi, single-handedly brought up Balraj, his younger brother Som and sister Rani. In an interview in 1999, Dad said: "The only thing I regret to this day is never seeing my father's face. There were no photographs — the trend of taking pictures didn't exist then. All I know about him was he was a handsome man, and my mother used to say whenever there was a wedding in the village, people would mistake him for the groom."

Early in life, Dad showed an inclination to battle the odds. He topped his class at the village junior school. But when he was old enough to attend secondary school, he discovered the nearest one was too far to reach by foot. Insisting on going to school by himself, Dad rode there each morning on horseback. He had a carefree yet frugal childhood, one that gave him a deep regard for the suffering of women, as he so closely observed the hardships his widowed mother had to endure.

A strong influence in Dad's life, his uncle suggested he join the army. He left for Kanpur when he was only 15 and enlisted. He worked as a clerk and would have stayed in the Army much longer had India not tragically been divided in 1947. Like millions of others, his entire family had to leave their village (now in Pakistan) overnight, and somehow make their way to India on foot or by train. There were many long months when Dad

Top (left): An early portrait of Dad, seen here with a friend.
Top (right): Younger brother, Som Dutt, lived with Dad in Mumbai in the 1950s. He also acted in films.
Left: Som and Puneeta Dutt and Hansraj Chibbar, whom we fondly called "Taayaji." Related to Dad on his paternal side, Taayaji was a father figure to Dad, playing a pivotal role in his early life.
Facing page: Kulwanti Devi, Dad's mother, was widowed at 23. She was a strong woman who raised her children despite many difficulties. Dad always sought her counsel and approval.

Thoroughly enjoying his time at Mumbai's Jai Hind College where he studied in the 1950s, Dad loved being surrounded by his many friends and together they would often go for outings near Bombay. Narang uncle (in striped shirt, *top left*) and MacMohan (the actor, *bottom left, extreme left*) remained friends till the end.

Facing page: Dad's character certificate dated 1948.

THE EDUCATICNAL CERTIFICATE.

This is to certify that <u>Bal Raj</u>   son of <u>L.Ragu Nath Datta</u>
of the D.A.V High School, Jhelum passed in the First Division
the Matriculation Examination of the PUNJAB UNIVERSITY held in
March 1945.

Passed also in <u>ONE</u> additional subject.

Dated 14.April 48.

Lieut.
ASC.Records(MT

CHARACTER CERTIFICATE.

This is to certify that No.3939 Civ.Clk. BALRAJ BATTA
S/O RAGHU NATH DATTA a Refugee from West Punjab (Jhelum) is
personally known to me.

He comes of a respectable Mohyal family and is a
promising young man with good physique and excellant character.

Dated 18 Mar.48.

Lt.-Colonel,
COMD.R.I.A.S.C. RECORDS (MT).

18 MAR 1948.
LUCKNOW.

Above: Dad hosting the popular *Lipton ke Sitaare* on Radio Ceylon (Asia's oldest radio station, established in 1923). He interviewed many movie stars including the famous singing star, Suraiyya. Mr Chandran, his ever-encouraging boss at Keymer's, is also seen here.
Left: With Dilip Kumar and Mr. Chandran during the Radio Ceylon days.
Facing page (left): Namrata's daughter once saw a picture of her grandfather and remarked how handsome he was. This lovely photograph shows him in a dreamy mood.
Facing page (right): With college friends.

didn't know where his mother and siblings were, and even feared they were lost in the chaos, looting and bloodshed raging on both sides of the Punjab. It was a frightening time and only after a long and arduous search was Dad finally reunited with his family whom he found in a refugee camp. Dad's family then lived together on the land they were given in compensation by the Government in a village called Mandoli, in Haryana. This became grandmother Kulwanti Devi's new home and she lived there till her last days.

In 1950, Dad left for Bombay to look for a job and study further. Before leaving for the big city, he arranged his sister Rani's marriage and made sure his brother Som was settled in school. Dad was not even 20 years old, but his life was already full of responsibility and turmoil. His family had lost everything at the time of Partition and now he had to help rebuild their lives.

Dad always had a strong sense of duty. He often told us if it weren't for the sacrifices he saw his young, widowed mother make in raising her three children and ensuring he had an education, he would never have achieved anything. In 1951, he worked as a radio host in Bombay while studying at Jai Hind College. An advertising company, D.J.

Keymer's, was looking for a new presenter to do interviews with film stars on Radio Ceylon in a show called *Lipton ke Sitaare* and chose Dad for the job. He always said what he enjoyed most about the Sunday interviews was reaching out to millions of people through his voice. In those days, Dad was in his first year of college and had to bunk a lecture to attend the radio audition. Mr Chandran, his boss at Keymer's, always believed in him and was most encouraging. He told Dad many times, "Balraj, time will wait for you."

Dad was paid Rs 25 for each interview and, in addition, he earned Rs 120 working at the B.E.S.T. bus depot as a checking clerk. Those were days of hard struggle. Dad did not have a home and each night he had to find a quiet corner to sleep, often ending up at the Simla Haircutting Saloon in Kala Ghoda, South Bombay. Between 9 P.M. and 7 A.M. when the saloon was closed to customers, he'd roll out his bedding and sleep on the floor. Sometimes he'd find himself an empty spot on a city pavement and settle there for the night. He attended classes at Jai Hind College in Churchgate in the morning and in the afternoon, worked at the B.E.S.T. bus terminus. He became a member of the Asiatic Library so he'd have a place to study. He told us how tough it was, but how much it helped to give him a strong sense of discipline. He was a good student and the teacher's pet. Tall and good looking, he attracted much attention at college in his white *kurta pajama* (of which he owned only two sets). He made sure to keep away from the girls though they tried to talk to him on the pretext that they needed his class notes. He always kept conversation with them strictly to the minimum, telling us how the college girls reminded him of his sister, Rani. He never flirted or had a relationship with anyone, thinking how terrible he'd feel if anyone had "flirted" with his own sister. He had to set an example. Dad was always an idealist!

In 1955, Dad graduated with honours in History. He often said his struggles were nothing in comparison to what his mother had to face. She remained his inspiration and he derived great strength from her. So in her own quiet way, our paternal grandmother was as unconventional as our more flamboyant maternal grandmother. Today, we three siblings believe we have imbibed the characteristics of both sets of grandparents. We follow our hearts, never compromise and don't really bother about convention, as long as we try to do the right thing.

In contrast to Dad's troubled and difficult childhood, Mom was brought up in great comfort,

Top (left and right): Mom's driver, Kasam *mama* and his wife Ameena *nani* were an important part of our family. They have now passed away.

Left: Mom loved saris and enjoyed designing them. She drew this sketch before she was married. The extravagant "peacock" design sari was never made.

Facing page: When she was 14, Mehboob Khan persuaded her to act in his 1943 *Taqdeer*, Mom's first role as lead heroine. Though she had worked in films at five, in her teens, she preferred studying over acting. But an offer by Mehboob *sahib* was difficult to refuse.

surrounded by domestic help and chauffeur-driven cars. She was very close to her father who was a softhearted and happy-go-lucky man. On the other hand, her mother, Jaddanbai, was a strong-willed lady, a pivotal figure in the household. Though much of Mom's strength was inherited from her mother, she was also in awe of her. After all, it was Jaddanbai who supported the family through her film career, whereas Mohan Babu, alas, wasn't good at business, despite having tried his hand at many things. Yet he was happy to be behind the scenes and remained a pillar of support for his wife who had enormous skill and creative talent. Her achievements were many at a time when having a professional life was rare for a woman. Chateau Marine, the building on Marine Drive in which she had a spacious ground-

floor flat, was the hub of many cultural activities and she actively promoted film-makers and musicians.

Sometimes we feel distressed to think Mom didn't really have much of a childhood. She may have lived in some luxury, but when she was only five she had to start working, albeit in her mother's movies. From that early age, and renamed "Baby Rani" for the screen, she continued working for the next 25 years. Mom did manage to continue her education till she was 14, attending school at Queen Mary's in Nanachowk, South Bombay where, because her name was Fatima, she was affectionately called "Fatty." A popular student, she excelled in drama and sports. Like her father, she once had dreams of becoming a doctor and shared with him a thirst for knowledge. She was a voracious reader, and absorbed herself in books and it was through reading that she learnt much about the world. But was the loss of childhood reflected in how – throughout her early years and later in adult life –

she collected dolls from all over the world until the time her children came along?

Everything changed dramatically for Mom when she was cast as the lead heroine of the aptly named *Taqdeer* (Fate, 1943), directed by the legendary Mehboob Khan. Mom was only 14 and reluctant to abandon her studies, harbouring dreams of becoming a doctor, a dream her father had not fulfilled. But Mehboob Khan thought of a ruse and asked her to come to the studio merely to watch Motilal on set. There, she was dressed in a sari by Mehboob Khan's wife, the actress Sardar Akhtar, and before Mom knew it, she was handed a page of dialogue and the great camerman Fardoon Irani, who coincidentally filmed her in her first film *Taalash-e-Haq*, took the shot. Mom impressed everyone. In an interview with Mohan Bawa (*Actors and Acting*, 1978), Mom recalled this incident, adding that it was the first time she had ever worn a sari and so kept tripping. One thing led to another and Mehboob Khan convinced her to opt for the movies. He believed the letter "N" was lucky for him and changed her name to "Nargis".

It proved fortuitous for him and for her as well. Soon hoardings bearing her new name in glittering letters were seen all over the country. Offers for film roles poured in and gradually Mom became the main provider for the family. From Baby Rani she had become the star Nargis and won a large fan following, but had lost her childhood forever. Mom, like Dad, had a strong sense of responsibility and felt happy when helping others. She was never resentful of her role as breadwinner at an age when so many of her friends were still enjoying the carefree pleasures of childhood.

Young Fatima, or "Baby" as she was fondly called, was escorted everywhere by her driver Kasambhai and personal maid Ameenabai. When Mom was already a big star, Dad was still at college. In an interview, he recalled how each morning, before attending college, he and his friends would sit on a Marine Drive parapet right opposite Chateau Marine where Mom lived, waiting for her white Railey car to go by. Obviously she never

Above (left): The only film in which Mom, Dilip Kumar and Raj Kapoor acted together was Meboob Khan's *Andaz* (1949).
Above (right): Mom acted as a village girl in many films.
Right: Filming on the Bombay shoreline.
Facing page: In *Taqdeer*, she was cast opposite the elegant and sophisticated star Motilal. They stayed friends through the years.

looked at them, but they waited for a glimpse of her and, as he put it, "especially her gorgeous car."

By the time she met Dad (probably sometime around 1956), she had acted in 46 films in the lead role. In 1955, when Dad was in his third year at college, Ramesh Saigal spotted him during a radio show in which Dad was interviewing Dilip Kumar at the Central Studio in Tardeo. Mr Saigal suggested Dad do a screen test, much to his surprise. One thing led to another and he found himself in a studio, wearing Dilip Kumar's shirt and trousers – a size too small – and carrying a walking stick in his hand, ready for his first screen test. Lights were beamed on his face and he was made to turn left, and then right, and then look straight ahead. This story made us all laugh as we could well imagine how utterly embarrassed Dad must have felt. He remembered the terrible dilemma when Mr Saigal, who had liked the screen test, sent his assistant to the college canteen to find him and give him a

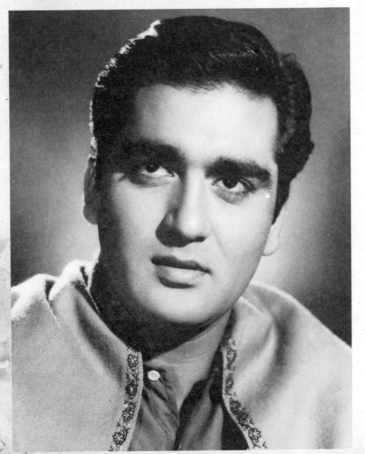

Above (left): Dad in *Amrapali* (1966).
Above (right): He finally gave up smoking when we children insisted he quit the habit.
Left: A still from Bimal Roy's *Sujata*, (1959).
Facing page: Mom's performances reflected her modern thinking. She was a woman way ahead of her time and that informed her non-theatrical, natural and modern acting style.

signing amount. Dad was still at college and had no plans to neglect his studies for any reason, and on top of that, he felt well settled in his job at Keymer's. It was his boss, Mr Chandran, who once again helped Dad come to a decision. He suggested Dad should continue studying, but also accept the film offer. Mr Chandran's advice was: "Let destiny take its course." Mr Saigal gave Dad an advance of Rs 150 to act in his first film, *Railway Platform* (1955). While Dad was making the movie, he also completed his degree. He was obliged to change his name, as another actor called Balraj (Sahni) was already well-known in the movies. Dad was happy to be called "Sunil," but refused to change his surname, as he was proud of his roots.

Coincidentally it was once again a Mehboob production, *Mother India* (1957) that completely changed Mom's life both professionally as well as personally. On the professional front, the making of the film marked the end of her long association with the RK Films' banner; on the personal front, she met the man she would soon marry. In *Mother India*, Mom plays Radha, the wife of Shyamu, a farmer, while Dad was cast as her rebellious son Birju. This was a role he got by chance, as initially he was to play the role of Radha's eldest son, Ramu (eventually played by Rajendra Kumar). But as luck would have it, at the last minute, the role of Birju fell into Dad's lap. Given the disparity in their status in the world of films — she was an established star and he, a newcomer — they did not strike up a friendship, though Mom was always known to

Above: *Mother India* premiered at Liberty Cinema on 25 October 1957. Mom's performance as Radha elevated her from actress to icon.
Top (right): Mehboob Khan knew Mom since she was a young child. She believed he was a man of vision and way ahead of his time. She always credited him for shaping her film career. From "Baby Rani," Mehboob Khan renamed her "Nargis," believing that names starting with the letter "N" were fortuitous.

interact with the whole unit effortlessly. She never had airs and was never stuck up. Dad always described Mom's presence as regal, "You couldn't say anything frivolous around her and whenever she entered the set everyone fell silent. It was her charisma. Yet with all this, she was unusually simple and unassuming."

Mehboob Khan paid Dad a monthly salary of Rs 800. It was a lot in those days and so he was never short of cash. Yet he chose to continue the radio interviews as well. For the first time, he splurged on himself by buying his first car – a Fiat with the number plate "1933". He loved the outdoors and drove around in his new car accompanied by friends including, Amarjeet, Kamal Kapoor, MacMohan, Bhagu and Mr Narang, who stood by him throughout his struggling days. They remained friends for life and together they enjoyed long drives to Pune, Kandhala, Mahabaleshwar, Delhi and Simla. Dad had by now moved into a small flat on Nepean Sea Road in Bombay where he lived with his sister Rani and her children. From time to time, his mother came from Mandoli in Haryana, with Som, his younger brother. A few years later, Som decided to live with Dad in order to pursue his studies in Bombay.

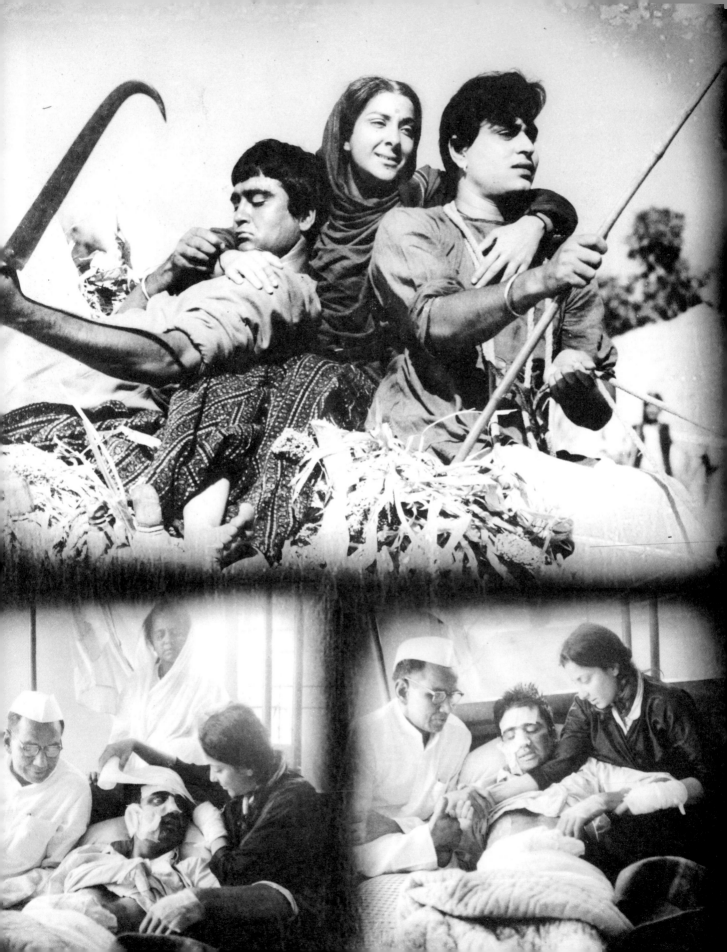

The Fire

A remake of his 1940 film *Aurat*, Mehboob Khan's *Mother India* was released in 1957. *Mother India* is a classic film and remains an important landmark in Indian cinema. In 1957, it was symbolic of the newly independent Indian nation, touching hearts wherever it was seen. It was an enormous box-office success, and Mom's performance as the film's heroine, Radha, won her both the Karlovy Vary and the Filmfare award for Best Actress.

In this powerful drama, Radha is a model heroine whose life becomes a repository of every kind of tragedy that might befall a woman. She is the wife of Shyamu (Raaj Kumar), a poor peasant farmer whose family gets trapped in an endless cycle of debt. Shyamu's arms are crushed in an accident, and no longer able to provide for his wife and children, he decides to leave the village in the dead of night. Radha finds herself all alone to provide for her young sons, face a merciless world and ward off the unwanted attentions of Sukhilala (Kanhaiyalal), the lecherous moneylender. Radha manages to stave off the moneylender's advances, and battling against the odds, she saves her children from starvation following a devastating flood. Through Radha's many trials, it is her ability to preserve a sense of dignity that becomes her greatest strength. Years pass and Radha's two sons, Ramu (Rajendra Kumar) and Birju (played by Dad), are now grown. Despite the fact that Birju, her delinquent son, is her favourite, he turns into a rebel and kidnaps the moneylender's daughter. Radha is ultimately forced to kill him to save the girl's honour.

On 1 March 1957, during the shooting of a dramatic fire scene, things went horribly wrong. Mom had been asked to use a double, but feeling sorry for the girl, she decided to do the stunts herself. In the scene, Radha has to run between burning haystacks, looking for her son, Birju. During the shoot, Mom became trapped in a circle of fire, and when the wind changed direction, she was unable to escape. Without a moment's hesitation, Dad ran into the raging flames and rescued her at great risk to his own life. His hands and face had serious burns and Mom's hands were badly scorched too.

They were then sent to convalesce in Mehboob Khan's house in the small town of Bilimora, not far from Umra, the Gujarati village where *Mother India* was being shot. Mom spent day and night looking after Dad, as he was in acute pain.

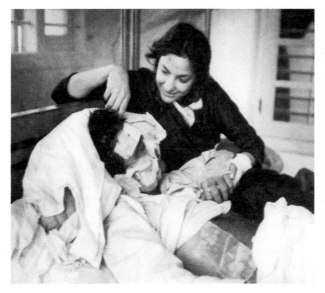

The fortnight they spent together was a turning point for them. It was during this time they fell in love. And so they decided to get married. In private and some secrecy, they were engaged on 12 March 1957. The world believed they had fallen in love because he had saved her, but Dad refuted the rumour many times, saying he hadn't rescued her because he was in love with her, and would have saved anyone in a similar predicament. He believed it was the right thing to do. Years earlier, when he had just arrived in Bombay and was strolling near the Gateway of India, he saw a man accidentally fall into the sea. Many people gathered to watch yet no one budged. Without so much as thinking, Dad jumped in and saved the man.

Dad told us how his love for Mom had grown and developed in the days and nights while she nursed him. Following the fire incident, he had the chance to discover her, not as the "filmstar Nargis," but as a generous and compassionate human being. This became more apparent when his sister Rani fell ill. She was living with Dad at the time and was suffering from tuberculosis. Mom took charge and made sure Rani had all the medical care required.

Dad later said what drew him to Mom was the selfless way she helped Rani. As a man who valued his family, he had always wanted a wife who would

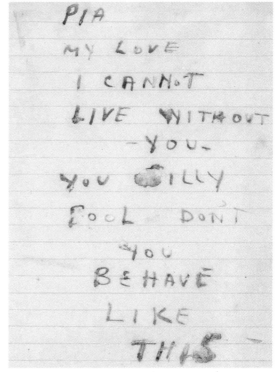

PIA
MY LOVE
I CANNOT
LIVE WITHOUT
—YOU—
YOU SILLY
FOOL DON'T
YOU
BEHAVE
LIKE
THIS—

This page (top): Saving Mom from a fire accident during the filming of *Mother India*, Dad suffered major burns. She nursed him day and night while he convalesced in Mehboob Khan's Bilimoria home in Gujarat, near the village of Umra where the filming of *Mother India* took place. By the time he recovered, they were in love.
Above: A note Dad once wrote to Mom during their courtship.
Facing page: Dad plays Birju, Radha's errant son in *Mother India*.
Preceding page 38: *Mother India* changed Mom and Dad's lives completely, both professionally and personally.

Above: A rare family photograph; (*Back row, l to r*) cousin Gopal, Dad's brother-in-law Balakrishna Bali, sister Rani Bali, Dad, Mom, Dad's brother, Som Dutt, and his wife Puneeta Dutt; (*Front row*) Cousin Sunita, Sanjay and Namrata. This was taken a day after Som Dutt's wedding in Ambala, 11 December, 1964.
Facing page: Mom was devastated by the death of her father in November 1947. Within a year of Mohan Babu's demise, her mother, Jaddanbai, passed away in July 1948.

care for his mother and siblings. His family had endured so much and Dad believed he needed a woman who would empathize with them. He told Mom he'd only marry her if his mother approved, as he didn't want to hurt her in any way. This was despite Grandmother telling Dad she had complete confidence in him, because she knew he would consider his family before arriving at any important decision.

Within a few months of their dramatic encounter, Dad proposed to Mom. He dropped her home one day in his new Fiat with its memorable number plate "1933" (he kept the car for many years purely for sentimental reasons). He was hesitant, repeating many times, "I have to ask you something, I have to tell you something." He believed this was a "do or die situation" and felt he would be shattered if she refused. He told us if Mom had rejected him

he would have left Bombay and gone back to his mother's village home in Haryana.

Years later, Dad recalled that day, describing his joy and relief: "I dropped her home and told her, 'I really like you and I want to marry you.' She didn't say anything to me. She walked out of the car and went inside her apartment building. And that was that. I didn't know how to face myself, I was miserable. The next day I went to work, and when I returned home, my sister Rani said '*Mubarak ho aapko,*' (Congratulations!). I asked 'Whatever for?'

And she replied, '*Unhone haan kar di hai*' (She has consented)." For a moment Dad didn't know what Rani was talking about. And then she said, "*Nargisji aayee thi* (Nargisji came over) and she has agreed."

Could Mom have refused him? She was a famous filmstar, but there was a big vacuum in her personal life. She lived for everyone else and had nothing to call her own. When her parents died, she was left with two brothers, Akhtar and Anwar Hussain, and their families to whom she was close. She looked after her nieces and nephews, helping them emotionally as well as financially. But her own life felt increasingly empty. She longed for a home and children of her own. She wanted a simple life, but didn't have one. Now, at last, she had the chance to make these dreams a reality.

How did Sunil Dutt, who was just a hopeful new actor in Bombay, have the confidence to propose to the hugely popular star Nargis, known throughout India and in many countries where Indian films were enjoyed? When Dad came to Bombay, he was a modest son of the soil; he knew no one and didn't have any friends. He came with nothing and managed to reach great heights whilst never abandoning his principles. Though life had sometimes been a struggle for Dad, things always managed to end well.

Dad had that same positive attitude when he proposed to Mom. There were many things that could have dampened his spirits, but they never mattered. He was a proud man who believed in himself. He gave Mom a great sense of security. After the release and international acclaim of *Mother India*, she had reached the highest point in an already illustrious career. She was ready to leave behind the world of fame and glory and lead the life of what she believed to be "a complete woman."

Despite their joy at the prospect of a life together, there were reasons they needed to keep their wedding plans a secret. The first was they happened to be playing mother and son in *Mother India* (the film had yet to be released), and secondly, director Mehboob Khan was unhappy about their romantic liaison because he thought the film would flop if news of their affair leaked out. The Indian public would never accept an on-screen mother and son getting married, albeit in real life. Another important reason was that Mom's family opposed the marriage. Her elder brother, Akhtar, was completely against it and so the only family member she could confide in was Anwar, who was more sympathetic. She told him, "We're going to get married, but I can't tell Akhtar Bhai. He will kill me."

Mom lost both her parents when she was 18. Her father passed away in November 1947 and within a year of Mohan Babu's demise, her mother, Jaddanbai, passed away in July 1948. Her brother Akhtar became the father figure in her life. He was incredibly protective about his sister and also managed her career. He knew Mom was considered by the 1950s among the top actresses and Dad was virtually a newcomer. Marriage was a huge step at this stage of her personal and professional life and Mom knew her brother would oppose it. Perhaps he felt Dad was trying to exploit Mom's fame and wealth. Akhtar uncle realized his mistake some years later and reconciliation came about when Sanjay was born in 1959.

Dad was an extremely proud man with a great deal of self-respect. He never wanted Mom to lack any comfort. He did not want her to accept a a more modest lifestyle for his sake

As Mom and Dad had no photographs of their wedding, Mom wittily created a wedding album showing Elvis Presley as the groom and Marilyn Monroe as the bride.

and so bought a large sprawling bungalow at 58 Pali Hill (in Bandra, a Bombay suburb). Dad couldn't actually afford the bungalow, but the owner, Manu Subedar, agreed to sell it to him on installment basis on 1 September 1957. They couldn't move into the Pali Hill house immediately because it was dilapidated and needed renovation. A short time later, it became their home.

Dad and Mom were married in a quiet ceremony on 11 March 1958 according to Arya Samaj rites. The wedding ceremony took place at the yet to be renovated Pali Hill bungalow. Mom wore a red and green sari for the occasion. Dad was in simple attire and wore a pink turban on his head. They were both 29 years old. The guests at the wedding reception held at the house of friends Shakuntala and her husband Virendra, were a few close friends, including Dad's sister Rani, cameraman Fardoon Irani and his wife, Gul, Dad's best friend Amarjeet, Mehboob Khan's assistant Chimankant Gandhi. Mehboob Khan did not attend the wedding as he was in the US preparing for the Oscar night (held on 26 March 1958).

At the time they were married, their marriage was a rare Hindu and Muslim union. People from all walks of life talked about the wedding and many were against it. Nargis was a superstar and many believed the marriage would never work. There were strong reactions and serious threats from both Hindus and Muslims, who asked questions like, "What religion will your children follow?" To which Dad replied, "They will follow the religion of humanity." And

Our Engagement

We became Engaged on <u>Tuesday - 12th March 1954 -</u>

Our Engagement Party

was held on <u>Tuesday - night after 12oclock</u>

at <u>Billimera - in one small room - with the moo</u> our guest —

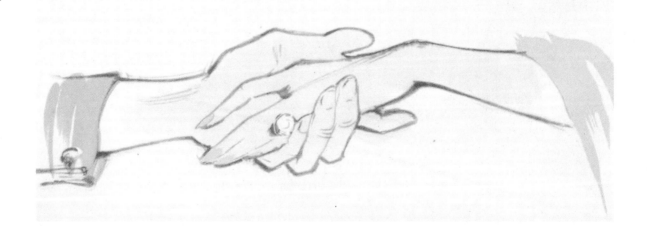

The Wedding

We were married on <u>11ᵗʰ day of March 1958</u>

at <u>Palli Hill Bandra Bombay -</u>

The Reception was held

at <u>Shakuntala's House — opposit Omar Park —</u>

and we had <u>One</u> — guests. Ruby

Pages from the wedding album created by Mom.

that's exactly what our parents taught us – to always be good human beings.

Life had completely changed for Mom after she met Dad. In those days, many actresses didn't retire after marriage and carried on working, but she was happy to leave behind the world of glamour and film. Mom wanted a new life and identity now that she was Mrs Sunil Dutt. In public, Dad always called her "Mrs Dutt" and she addressed him as "Dutt *sahib*." In private, they called each other "Jio."

Life must have been difficult for Mom in the early days of marriage. Leaving her family could not have been easy nor facing new hardships. From the comfort of her four-bedroom apartment on Marine Drive – and before they moved to the Pali Hill bungalow – they lived in a tiny apartment in a building called "Stardust" on Nepean Sea Road. It was a small one-bedroom flat, which they shared with Dad's mother, sister Rani, her children, a domestic help and a dog. And yet, Mom never thought twice about abandoning her belongings in her grand Marine Drive apartment.

There were other aspects of her new life she knew nothing about. For example, she had never

Above and facing page: Children don't often think their parents are capable of romance. The selfish assumption is that parents exist to nurture us kids. Writing this book allowed us to glimpse into the way Mom and Dad experienced small and big moments of their lives. It was so moving to read Mom describe their quiet and discreet engagement: "Our engagement party was held on Tuesday (12 March 1957) after 12 o' clock at Bilimoria in our small room with the moon as our guest." In 23 years of marriage, our parents were the happiest when together. They also made sure to give each other ample space to grow and develop as individuals.

cooked before, and in later life, Dad would often take credit for making sure Mom learned how to cook. "I was the one who encouraged her. I'd have competitions in the house and ask Rani to cook a dish and then Mrs Dutt would cook a dish. That's how she developed an interest in cooking!"

Within a year of their marriage, they moved to their newly renovated home at 58 Pali Hill in Bandra. Theirs was now the life Mom had so wanted. Dad would go to the studio everyday and she would be busily happy at home. When Mom moved from her maternal home, she made sure to take with her two special people: her driver Kasambhai and maid Ameenabai, whom we fondly called "Ameena *nani*" (granny Ameena). She had looked after Mom since Mom's childhood and all

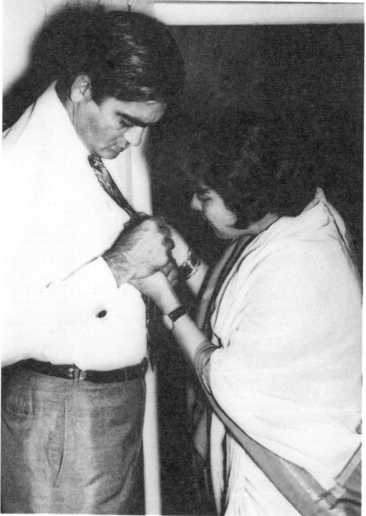

Top: Our cherished home at 58 Pali Hill where we spent some glorious years.
Bottom: Years later we realized that Dad was utterly lost without Mom.
Facing page: Mom and Dad dedicated this photograph to a dear friend.

To Gen. Bijji & family with affectionate regards

Mrs. Sunil Dutt

through her film career. Ameena *nani* had no children of her own and Kasambhai and she loved Mom like a daughter. Ameena *nani* lived with us until the day she died and was the grandmother we never knew.

Mom chose to act in only one film (*Raat aur Din*) after she was married and this was because it was produced by her elder brother, Akhtar. *Raat aur Din* took 10 years to be completed and won her in 1968 the Urvashi Award for Best Actress (later called the National Award). By then, Mom had happily abandoned the pancake and make-up of the silver screen for a light dash of lipstick, eyeliner and

impeccably manicured nails. Choosing this new way of life was no big sacrifice for her, as she had always preferred simplicity. She almost always wore white cotton and was famously known as the "lady in white." Mom once explained why she came to be called so. When her father died, following the custom, she wore white in mourning. Eight months later, her mother passed away and in bereavement she was in white again. By then she had grown to love wearing white saris and soon her fans expected her to see her only in white. She obliged, not wanting to disappoint them. She did wear different colours, but Mom's image in white remained etched

on the minds of her fans. The simplicity and no-fuss of her white cotton saris was in great part well-suited to her down-to-earth nature.

Sometimes Dad could be a difficult man. If he had something in mind, it had to be done his way. He was demanding and yet Mom was happy to be the perfect wife. She was in love with him, and her love was strong and unwavering. In addition, she was also attracted to Dad because he was such a good-looking man. Years later, when my daughter, Saachi, saw early photos of her grandfather, she couldn't believe her eyes. She'd tell him in an astonished tone, "Wow! Is that you, *Nanaji*? No wonder Grandma fell for you."

Dad had great qualities. He was a man of principles; honest and never devious like many people in this world. He never hid the fact that he was living in a one-bedroom flat and didn't have the sort of money she was used to. She knew it and that never bothered her. Dad was never pretentious and was the kind of person who made everyone feel secure and safe. Nothing could go wrong if he was by your side. They respected each other deeply and built a new life together based on strong foundations.

Yet Mom and Dad had incredibly different personalities. Dad was soft-spoken and quiet. On the other hand, Mom would call a spade a spade, never mincing her words. I remember when we were driving home one day and Mom saw a man relieving himself against a street wall. She stopped the car and shouted at him. He was so embarrassed. I don't think he ever forgot this incident for the rest of his days. There were many such incidents. Mom was gutsy and often described herelf as a fighter. She didn't care about status either. She was straightforward and this often went against her. Dad was extremely diplomatic and a thorough gentleman. If Mom went out, Dad would make us laugh by saying, "The house is so quiet, I can't hear any yelling and screaming – it must mean Mom isn't at home." Amongst us siblings, Sanjay used to get yelled at the most.

Top: Brother Akhtar Hussain.
Bottom: Mom proudly received the Karlovy Vary Best Actress Award for *Mother India*. She was also the first actress to be decorated with the Padmashree award (1958).
Facing page: Accepting the Urvashi Award (now called the National Award) from the President, the late Dr Zakir Hussain, Delhi, 1968, for *Raat aur Din*. In *Raat aur Din*, she plays a woman with a split personality. Produced by A.A.N Productions (brothers Akhtar, Anwar and Nargis), this was her last film.

Together At Last

Above: Sanjay with Dad.
Facing page: Sanjay's baby book.
Preceding page 54: The family was complete when Priya was born on August 28 1966. We recently found a picture of us three with Mom which she had captioned "the lioness and her cubs".

anjay was born on 29 July 1959, within a year of their marriage. His birth transformed Mom. She could finally put away her collection of dolls that she had kept all her life, as she now had the baby she longed for. Then on 5 January 1962 I was born and named Namrata — though everyone in the family called me Anju to rhyme with Sanju! And, finally, Priya was born on 28 August 1966. The family was complete. From Nargis and Sunil Dutt, they became simply Mom and Dad.

We were, and still are, a close and supportive family. We have always spent a lot of time together and this was thanks to the many strict rules Dad imposed while we were growing up. He made sure

he gave us a lot of personal time and love, and didn't want us to be spoilt by too much luxury. In the bungalow there was only one air-conditioned room (which doubled up as a library). Mom and Dad had their room and we had ours. But each night we would all sleep in the air-conditioned library — *gadda daal ke* (laying down mattresses on the floor). Priya used to sleep between Mom and Dad, and then there was me and Sanjay. Dad thought it was important we had a strong bond between us,

Date: 29th JULY 1959   WEDNESDAY

This was the
most important day of my life.
I arrived at 2-45 p.m.   o'clock -
at BREACH CANDY HOSPITAL + NURSING HOME - BOMBAY.

Here are the autographs
of
Father _____ Mother 7. D-tt.

Doctor _____   Nurse
                      Mary D'Monte.
P. m. mehta.   June Squirrell
(ANESTHETIC).

Birth

We proudly present

(Miss KAAJAL. ℬ. DUTT)   (MISS KAAJAL DUTT) - SUNILA DUTT
Baby's full name   MISS NAMRATA DUTT

Why we chose this name   Because it is a very unusual and a

sweet name - changed to Sunila - people thought Kaajal very unusual.
but Finally it is "NAMRATA" at Movie Store they call her Anju

Born   1962   JANUARY FRIDAY the 5th   10 hours 9 min. a.m.
         year   month   day   hour

Above: When Namrata was born she was named "Kaajal." Mom explains in the baby book why they decided to change the name.
Mom was fond of preserving photo albums, baby books and scrapbooks. It was as if, intuitively and unconsciously, she wanted something of our family history recorded.
Facing page: Priya's baby book. She was named Priyadarshini after Indira Gandhi.

Birth Information

was born on _____Sunday_____ the ___28ᵗ___ day of ___August___ , 19_66_

at ___12·09___ o'clock ~~P.M.~~ at ___the Breach Candy___ ~~Home~~ Hospital
 A.M.

City ___Bombay___ County_____ State ___Maharashtra___

Autographs

Doctor _____Burjisdastur_____

Nurses _____Be Ayesha Muldewwalla_____

Father _____[signature]_____
              BALRAJ DUTT

Mother _____Mrs. Fatima Sunil Dutt · (Nargis)_____

I

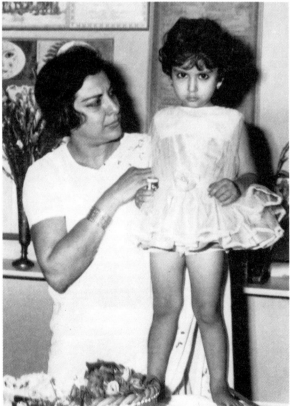

Top: Family and friends celebrate Namrata's birthday.
Above: Sanjay and Namrata share the birthday cake.
Left: Celebrating Priya's birthday.
Facing page: One day, Dad came home from a shoot with a bloodstain on his shirt. We children were terrified, fearing that he had been hurt. Calm returned when we were explained the stain was only make-up.

especially as he was often away on film shoots. Dad was a strict disciplinarian, but we could get away with blue murder as far as Mom was concerned. We had learned that there was no challenging Dad's rules. For example, there was only one TV in the house, and the family would watch it together. No phones were allowed in our bedrooms either. And we had to be back home before sunset, no matter what.

Mom gave up anything that might have come in the way of her children and her. A producer came one day with a blank cheque, asking her to act in his film. She laughed and sent him away saying she was currently working in three films, and they were called "Sanju, Anju and Priya." Mom was the entire focus of our lives. The house resounded with her voice, shouting at us, telling us to come inside for dinner if we were playing outdoors and screaming at us till we finished our homework. At other times she would be preoccupied and busy in arranging our birthday parties. We lived a happy, content and normal life. None of us knew her as the actress Nargis and she never talked about her identity as a star. The only habit she had that was mildly irritating to Dad was her *paan*-eating. She loved a fresh-leaf *paan*, but we kids didn't share that particular craving. She was a fun-loving, happy-go-lucky, straightforward Mom, who loved her family unconditionally. If we were in a school play, she would sometimes direct the play and teach the class how to act. She knew the principal of our school and occasionally used to help out there too. She was blissful being a mother, wife, homemaker and social worker.

Above: Playing with Namrata.

Left: Photograph taken by Dad in 1959 when Sanjay was a few months old. Mom seems amused to see our pet retriever, Prince, enthusiastically showering his affection on baby Sanjay.

Facing page (top): Mom was nearly always in saris, but sometimes she would wear a *salwar kameez*. Her favourite watch wasn't a delicate ladies' wristwatch, but a man's watch. In tune with her no-nonsense attitude towards many things, Mom liked the unfussy look of a man's watch. Sanjay was around two and a half and Namrata was six months old.

Facing page (bottom left): Our picnics at Powai Lake were the highlight of our childhood. Little did Priya and Dad realize that even years later they would share so many life experiences.

Facing page (bottom right): When Mom was pregnant with Sanjay, she vowed in the name of Imam Jaffer that if she were granted a healthy baby, she would offer two *kundas* (earthen pots) filled with *kheer* and *puris* each year. This tradition (known as *Hazrat Imam Jaffar Sadiq Ale Salaam ki niyaz*) was followed in her parental home. Mom's uncle, his wife and our cousins continue this tradition to this day. In addition, our cousins offer "*alaam*" in Sanjay's name each year at Moharram (this was also followed by Mom to protect her first-born).

Above: Perched on the family car are Sanjay and Namrata, 1962.
Left: A family holiday in Kashmir with Mom, her niece Zahida, Sanjay and Namrata.
Facing page (top): Picnics at Powai Lake, northern Mumbai, were another treat. In the 1960s, Powai Lake was quite deserted and so Mom and Dad escaped being surrounded by fans.
Facing page (centre): Mom was very fond of her nieces and they frequently accompanied us on our outings. Mom and Shahida, Zahida and Rehana sit in the rear of the car.
Facing page (bottom): Mom seen here with Sanjay who was 12, Namrata, 10 and Priya, 6.

Being the youngest of the family, Priya was extremely close to Mom. She followed her everywhere. Dad was the typical working father, always coming home late from filming, sometimes at two or three in the morning, if he happened to be working a double shift. But when he got home, no matter what time it was, he would wake us up. Mom used to shout at him saying we had school the next day and needed to sleep. But he insisted, "When else will I see them?" So he'd wake us up and there would be lots of hugging and kissing and rolling about on the bed.

Life was also hugely enjoyable and we did
many things together as a family, including
swimming, horse riding and going on picnics. We
had a Mercedes van, which Mom had fitted with a
fridge and little sofa that could be converted into a
bed. Every weekend we would go for picnics with
Rehana (Mom's niece) and her husband Amarjeet
(Amarjeet was Dad's oldest friend who later
married Rehana) and other friends. Amarjeet uncle
would bring *biryani*, Dad used to marinate chicken
and Mom would barbecue it. Our favourite picnic
spots were at Tulsi Lake, Madh Island and Powai
Lake, near Bombay. In those days, there were no
crowds milling around and no fans or onlookers in
sight. We would have a great time.

Other big family occasions were our New Year
parties. This celebration coincided with the
anniversary of Ajanta Arts, the film production
company Mom and Dad had started on 1 January
1960. The extended family, friends, acquaintances
and the entire staff working at Ajanta Arts joined in.
There was Dilip (Kumar) uncle and Saira (Banu)
aunty, our neighbours for over 40 years and who
were like family to us. The other friends who came
included Rajendranath, Mukri, B.B. Bhalla and Raaj
Grover; Mom's nieces, Zahida and Rehana, and
Amarjeet, Mom's nephew Sarwar Hussain (who was
the Manager of Ajanta Arts and later became Dad's
private secretary), Anwar uncle, who was always
associated with Dad's movies, Som uncle, Vinod
Khanna, Shammi aunty, Ranjeet and Waheeda
Rahman. We kids were allowed to join in too. Dad
would announce into a microphone, "Everyone
must say a few words about this event," and then the
microphone would be passed around. It was a ritual.
Everyone had to speak, including the children, and
we would describe our impressions of the party.
Dad continued this ritual till the very end.

Throughout our childhood, Dad kept us
strictly away from the film world. Our parents
wanted us to study hard and were passionate about
our education. Despite the fact Dad travelled a lot,
he insisted on keeping a track on what we were
taught at school. He'd come home, sit us down and

ask, "What did you learn this week? What poems
have you learned? I must hear everything. Recite the
poems to me." So Mom and Dad made us stand in
elocution pose and recite.

It was Mom who checked our homework on a
day-to-day basis. She would make it a point to be
home in time to have lunch with us each and every
day. Mom also spent a lot of time with her nieces,
Zahida and Rehana, and close friends including the
actress Shammi Rabadi. Shammi aunty and Mom
had known each other since their acting days and
their friendship was strong. Shammi aunty once told
us a funny story. She and Mom had to attend a
funeral to offer condolences. Mom quickly wore a
white sari and rushed over with Shammi aunty to
the person's home, only to realize later that they
had, in their haste, gone to the wrong house. And
the friend they believed to be dead and enroute to
the graveyard, opened the door with a big and
welcoming smile. They did this kind of thing often.
They were a lethal combination and their pranks
reminded us of Lucy Ricardo (Lucille Ball) and

Left: Mom and Dad were proud of having started the Ajanta Arts film company on 1 January 1960.

Bottom (left): Sanjay and Namrata at an Ajanta Arts awards ceremony.

Bottom (right): To coincide with the Ajanta Arts anniversary and to welcome the New Year, they held a huge party each year. Friends and everyone working at Ajanta Arts joined in.

Facing page (top): Shammi aunty, Mom and Puneeta aunty (Dad's younger brother Som Dutt's wife) look through a family album at a party held at home.

Facing page (bottom): Shammi aunty with Dad. Coincidentally when Shammi aunty was born she was named "Nargis."

Top: With Grandma. Being a shy lady, Grandma was extremely embarrassed when Dad forced her to speak at an Ajanta Arts celebration.
Bottom: A rare still showing Dad and the best comedians of Hindi cinema (*l to r*) Mukri, Johnny Walker and Mehmood.
Facing page (top): Shammi Kapoor joined in an annual Ajanta Arts' party, which was like a cultural programme with singers and poetry recitals.
Facing page (bottom left): The Iranis were witnesses at our parents' wedding. Fardoon Irani was the cameraman for all of Mehboob Khan's films.
Facing page (bottom right): Amarjeet was Dad's old and dear friend who later married Mom's niece Rehana.

Top: (*l to r*) Vinod Khanna, Raj Khosla, Asha Bhonsle, Premnath, Dad, R.D. Burman, Anand Bakshi.

Left: In 1967, Namrata gives the clap for the *mahurat* shot of *Mann ka Meet*. Our paternal Grandmother looks on.

Facing page (top): Comedian Mukri, who starred with Dad in *Mother India*, remained a firm friend, as did Kishore Kumar. Dad and Kishore Kumar had a rollicking time in *Padosan* (1968), and were always prone to clowning around whenever they met.

Facing page (bottom): Dad relished the opportunity of hearing the great *ghazal* singer Begum Akhtar, who was said to have been inspired by Jaddanbai. One of the last performances Dad attended was of Pakistani *ghazal* singer, Farida Khanum, who sang his favourite *ghazal*, *Aaj jaane ki zidd na karo*. They discovered they were both great fans of each other.

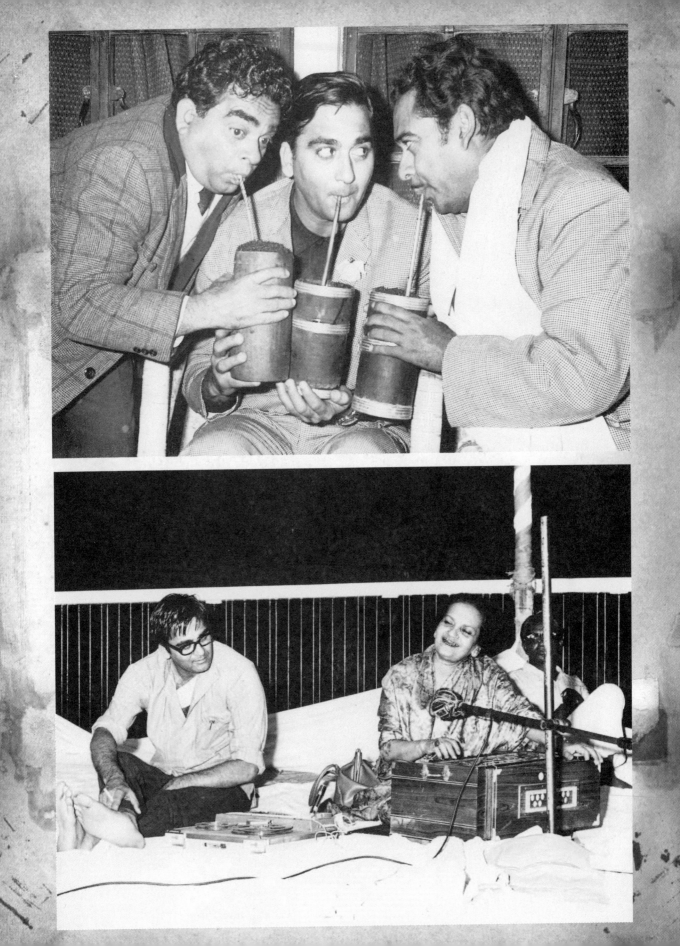

Ethel Mertz (Vivian Vance) in the series *I Love Lucy*. Mom and Shammi aunty were very similar to these two imaginative people who had a knack of getting into trouble.

Mom always stood up for her friends. She was a loyal friend, and everyone who knew her, adored her loving nature and humility. She never thought twice about helping anyone in need. She was selfless and never failed her friends. She used to say, "Even if you can't share happy times with your friends, you must stand by them in their time of loss or sorrow, because it is then that they need you the most."

Mom and Dad often travelled abroad together, sometimes on film shoots or to attend events and film festivals. They toured in many parts of India with the Ajanta Arts Welfare Troupe – the setting up

Above: Mom and Dad had great admiration and respect for Pandit Nehru who was also a family friend.
Facing page: The Ajanta Arts Welfare Troupe shows were held to entertain the Indian Army *jawans* in the border areas following the wars and conflict of 1962, 1965 and 1971. Dad helps Waheeda Rahman onto the stage before the show starts. Kishore Kumar, who was also present, was suddenly overcome with stage fright.

of the Ajanta Arts Welfare Troupe was yet another proof of their social commitment. Following the Chinese Aggression in 1962, Dad set up the Welfare Troupe later that same year. The idea came to him when he went to meet Pandit Nehru and present him with a cheque for Rs 1 lakh for the National Defence Fund. He asked Panditji if there was any other way he might be of use. Panditji told him many *jawans* (soldiers) were living in cold and harsh conditions and needed entertainment to boost their

morale, as they were so far from home. There were no transistor radios in those regions at the time. To entertain the soldiers, Dad (often accompanied by Mom) would travel to remote areas taking with him actors and singers, including Lata Mangeshkar, Kishore Kumar and Waheeda Rahman. Indira Gandhi encouraged him to continue supporting the *jawans* in this way when she came to power on 19 January 1966. Despite their tremendous commitment to work, they gave us so much quality time. We never once felt their absence nor did we ever feel alone. In 1971, Mom and Dad had a difficult time when *Reshma aur Shera* was released. This was a film Dad had produced, directed and acted in. It won three National awards: Waheeda Rahman (Best Actress), Jaidev (Best Music Director), and Ramachandra Singh (Best Cinematography). Dad even entered the film in the Foreign Language film section of the Oscars. But *Reshma aur Shera* failed dismally at the box-office. It was then Dad taught us the importance of humility.

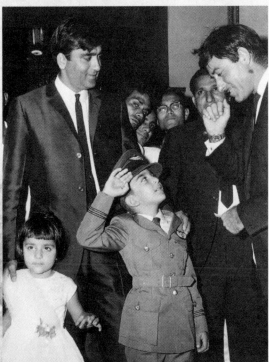

Top: Sanjay joins in an Ajanta Arts Welfare Troupe show held for the *jawans*.
Above: Actor/director B.B. Bhalla dressed as a woman to entertain the *jawans*.
Left: Sanjay and Namrata meeting Raaj Kumar.
Facing page (top): The ever-popular Lata Mangeshkar performs at a show organized by the Ajanta Arts Welfare Troupe.
Facing page (bottom): Kishore Kumar finally overcame his stage fright by standing behind Dad and singing. Dad duly lip-synched the song. The duo had great practice in this technique, having perfected it in *Padosan*.

Top: Dad visiting an army outpost.

Bottom: Dad was deeply humbled to meet soldiers who had been injured. He had great respect for the brave men who risked their lives for our country.

Facing page (top): On holiday from boarding school, Sanjay joined Dad during an Ajanta Arts Welfare Troupe show at Jassore, Bangladesh on 29 January 1972.

Facing page (bottom): Captain Gupta and Raaj Grover (with walking stick) were Dad's close friends. Whenever Dad made a friend, it was for life. Raaj Grover also worked for Ajanta Arts and was involved in four films produced by the company.

Above: Sanjay's first screen appearance was in *Reshma aur Shera*, as a *qawwali* singer.
Left: Waheeda Rahman and Dad on location in Rajasthan for *Reshma aur Shera*. This film was a great boost to the careers of Rakhee, Ranjeet and Amrish Puri.
Facing page: Mrs Gandhi congratulating Dad when he was awarded the Padmashree in 1968.

They couldn't afford anything "extra" during that period, but didn't want us to know our home had been mortgaged. It was a dark phase in Dad's life and he owed a lot of money to financiers.

The film was selected for technical excellence and Dad was invited to attend the Oscars and film festivals in Berlin and Tashkent. He needed a new film print, but the financier refused to pay the Rs 10,000 required. So he was forced to send a worn and badly scratched print. This really hurt him, but he accepted it as destiny. Dad later told us about those terrible days when he would find Mom darning socks and school uniforms because they couldn't afford to buy us new clothes. He described how Mom used to deal with those trying times: "In my wife's attitude, I found neither condemnation nor complaint. She went about her daily business

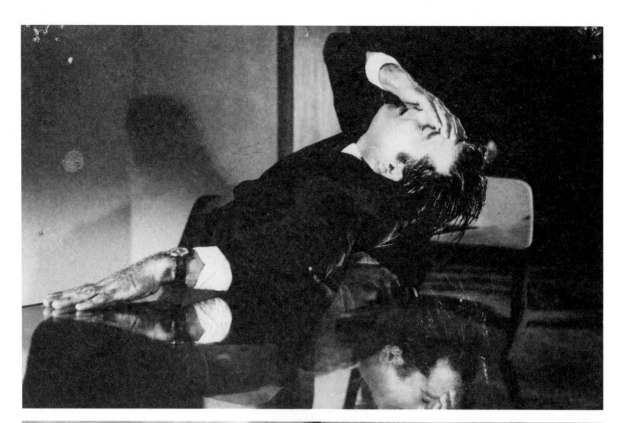

Left: Dad plays a dacoit in *Mujhe Jeene Do* for which he won the Filmfare Best Actor Award, 1963. This film was one of the early movues set in the world of dacoits, and no doubt triggered the interest in the many other dacoit films that followed.

Below: Waheeda Rahman in *Mujhe Jeene Do*, performing the wonderful song by Sahir Ludhianvi, *Raat bhi hain kuch bheegi* with music by Jaidev. This song sung by Lata Mangeshkar was the most popular song of the film.

Facing page (top and bottom): When Dad decided to direct a film, he opted for an experimental approach and made *Yaadein*, which has a single character carrying the entire narrative. This was the first "one" character film ever made in India and it received much critical acclaim.

without any resentment. She had a way of accepting life and it showed in how she brought up the children." Mom had a habit of collecting coins in a tall box. Dad told us one day, when they were really broke and had no money even for household expenses, Mom opened the box, threw all the coins on the bed and started counting. It took her a couple of hours to count all the change, but she was delighted to find they now had enough money to last the next 30 days. I think it was because of her positive attitude that none of us experienced what our parents were really going through at the time.

Sanjay once threw a tantrum about something he wanted Dad to buy for him. He was too young to understand there were certain things we simply couldn't afford. But Sanjay would not relent. Dad got really upset. He made us get into the car and, along with Mom, drove us to the slums near the airport. He said, "You know, you have a grand roof over your heads. Just look at these children." He was trying to tell us we should be grateful to God for everything we had. This left a deep impression on us. To this day, we know if we can't have something we want, we can't have it and that's all there is to it.

Sanjay could be really naughty when he was a boy. Perhaps it was because he knew, in Mom's eyes, he could do no wrong. When Dad was once shooting in Kashmir, she took Sanjay with her to visit him. Just to annoy Mom and to get her attention, Sanjay started pestering her, saying he wanted to smoke a cigarette. Sanjay recalls the incident with much regret: "Because I was still so young, she got mad at me. Dad came from the shoot and said, 'If he wants to smoke let him smoke.' Dad lit a cigarette and put it in his mouth and told me, 'Do exactly as I do.' He inhaled the smoke, and

Top (left): Mom loved taking Sanjay with her to parties and weddings, and he was proud to be by her side. When he was sent off to boarding school at 10, he was traumatized by this separation.
Top (right): (*l to r*) Actresses Madhumati and Kumkum at a party at our Pali Hill bungalow. Sanju is busy trying to grab Mom's attention by tugging at her sari *pallu*.
Right: Sanjay was at boarding school at Lawrence School, Sanawar, and on Founders' Day the family visited him. Here he is with Namrata, 9, and Priya, 5.
Facing page: Rakhee's performance in *Reshma aur Shera* (1971) won her much acclaim. When she married Gulzar *sahib*, Dad performed her *kanyadaan* and Priya and Namrata were bridesmaids. S. D. Burman (*far left*) also graced the occasion.

passed the cigarette to me thinking I'd choke and throw it away. But I smoked the whole thing. I must have been six years old."

The syndrome of the adored child who gives the most joy and the greatest heartbreak would never be easily resolved. Mom and Sanjay were especially close and he used to take complete advantage of her. She spoiled him utterly till they decided his growing up in Bombay would bring his downfall. And this was something Sanjay sensed too: "They sent me to a boarding school in Sanawar, near Simla, and I think it was the best thing that could've happened to me. I remember when they took me

there – I was so shattered when they left me. That night I distinctly remember hearing Mom's voice coming from outside the dorm. I opened the door, but she wasn't there. She was absolutely special to me. I cried like hell for days and days. She was equally shattered to have sent me away from home. But I agree, growing up in Bombay would have ruined me. Both Mom and Dad wanted me to be

Darling Son Sanjay -

After I left you in school I was terribly disturbed - You were crying and I was feeling very bad - Sanjay - I know my boy that you must be missing home and me, we miss you too - the house is empty without you - but Sanjay you must try to understand that it is for your own good - You will be a good student - and study well over there - You results there are much better than what they were in Bombay Now you have promised to do even better and I promise I will come to see you every month - You know you are our only Son and we have great hopes on you - You must study hard and become a big man so that you can look after us in our old age.

So no more crying - pay attention
in your class - there is plenty of
time for you to play - Please Sanjay
for my sake be more attentive
in you class, you must do this
much to please you mother -
I hope you secure better marks,
Be a good boy, dont give
any chance to your teachers to
be angry with you any time -
Promise me that you will
study well - look after yourself
you are a big boy - we love
you too too much - you know
that - God Bless you and keep
you away from all harm -
With all my love and kisses
to you -
Your loving
Mama.

Mom was heartbroken whenever she had to leave Sanjay at Sanawar.
She would write letters to him frequently with details of what was
happening in our lives in Bombay.

more humble and more independent. In the beginning, I didn't understand that and felt rejected. I was only 10 years old."

Sanjay wrote tearful letters from boarding school, and Mom and Dad sent him consoling replies. Between the lines you could sense their agony at having sent him away. Mom would take every opportunity to visit him. His early sad letters made Mom cry so much.

But the most painful thing for Sanjay was going back to boarding school after the term break. The train to Simla was always the most difficult journey for him. Gradually things improved once he joined senior school where he had a group of close friends. Then he began writing home saying he never wanted to be at any other school, ever, and Lawrence School was the best. Sanjay recalls, "I used to spend time with Mom whenever possible. She would come to the school on Founders' Day. And the holidays, which came round twice a year, we'd

go abroad with Mom and Dad. It was the only way we could be together, going on our European holidays every year."

One of my most vivid memories of Mom was her coming to school to pick me up. I used to go from Bandra to town every day and though Dad didn't really like me commuting so far. But as our cousins were at Cathedral and John Connon School (Fort, South Bombay), so I had to study there too. The school was 15 minutes away from Akhtar uncle's house, so I'd have lunch there and then return to class. Then Mom would pick me up at 3:30 in the afternoon and we'd come home together. This was our routine until the day Priya joined Cathedral. Then Mom felt Priya was too young to travel so far, so we were admitted into a school in Bandra.

During the time Mom was looking for a new school for us, she happened to be on the advisory board of the State Telephone Department. One of

Above: Mom's work for the Spastics Society meant a lot to her. On this particular day, "the King of the Ring" and social activist, Muhammad Ali, came to visit.
Right: Mom with Mithu Alur, Chair of the Spastics Society school.
Facing page: Mom had a great ease with children with special needs and whenever she had the opportunity, she would speak publicly of what could be done to help them.

the schools she visited needed new telephone lines, so they said "Mrs Dutt, we'll take your daughters if you get us two phone lines." She refused, telling them they could not impose any conditions on her. She was always straightforward in everything she did. She then admitted us into A.F. Petit Girls' High School awhere she happened to get along very well with Mrs Bharucha, the school principal. Our new school was a five-minute walk from home, so we'd come back for lunch and Mom would be waiting for us. Our school days were fantastic. We were so happy. Some years later, when I was studying at Sophia Polytechnic, Mom was working at the Spastics Society of India in Colaba, South Bombay. And whenever she had the time, she'd pick me up after college and we'd go home to Bandra, dropping off three of my friends on the way.

When we were young, Priya remembers never leaving Mom's side: "I was extremely close to her. I was at an age when I wanted to be with her all the time while Namrata and Sanjay wanted to spend time with their friends. I think it was great for Mom to have me there and it was great to be with her. She would even take me to attend weddings! She'd tell me we're going to see the bride and we'll get damn good food to eat and bribe me to come along. I was happy just to be with Mom."

Though Mom had given up working in films, she was busy with social work. Helping others who

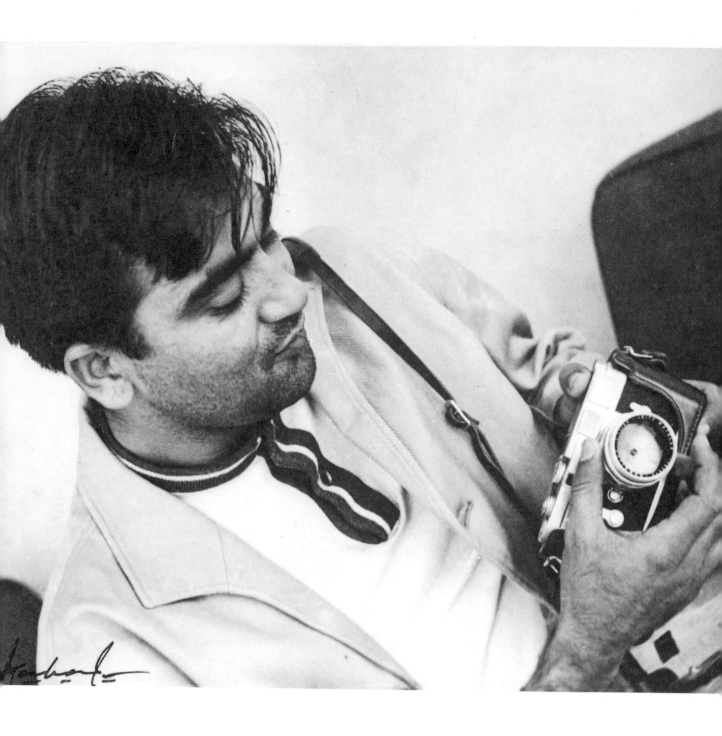

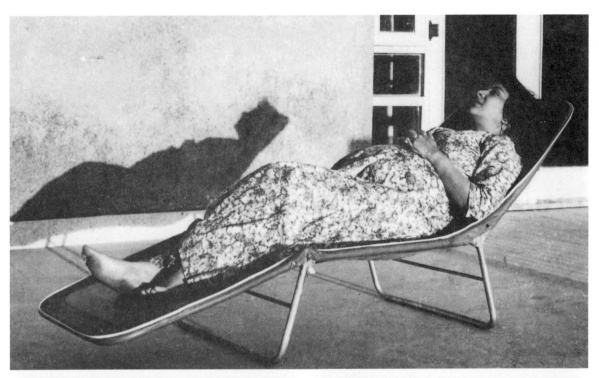

This page: Mom relaxing when pregnant. Sanjay when he was a toddler (*left*) and in his teens (*above*).

Facing page: Dad loved his Nikon and Hasselblad cameras and regarded them among his prized possessions. He carried his Nikon everywhere and learnt a lot about photography from his friend Jaywant Ulhal. Later he shared his passion for photography with Dayanita Singh (Sanjay's school friend from Sanawar), who is like a family member to us. The pictures on this page and facing page (top right) are taken by Dad.

were in need was a crucial feature of her life. Besides her commitment to the Ajanta Arts Welfare Troupe, she was involved in many fund-raising activities and charities. Perhaps the most important of her commitments was her work at the Spastics Society of India, founded in Bombay by Dr Mithu Alur. Dr Alur had asked Mrs Indira Gandhi for help to set up a school for spastic children and she suggested to her the names of people who might help. Aware of Mom's social work, Indira Gandhi added Mom's name to Dr Alur's list. Indira Gandhi was aware of Mom's social work and so added her name to the list. When the time came, Mom told Dr Alur she wanted to be more than a patron and do hands-on work to help the children. The Spastics Society was housed opposite Colaba's Afghan Church and initially started with four children, one being Dr Alur's own daughter, Malini. Priya and I went occasionally with Mom to Colaba, where on most afternoons, she worked with the children. This was, and continues to be, rare for a celebrity to voluntarily give up time and energy to create social change, without seeking any self-publicity.

Mom used to tell us how utterly frustrating it was for a spastic child to have an intelligent brain in a disobedient body. She would explain to us the difference between spastics and the mentally retarded. If she were alive today, she would have done her best to bring change in attitudes towards children with disabilities, who clearly should not be socially excluded. Mom became more and more involved in the Spastics Society, later helping them to get land from the Government to set up a full fledged school in Bandra.

It was also clear that Mom had inherited some of her mother's business genes. It was she who realized we needed a steady source of income, given the uncertain and sporadic earnings coming from Dad's work in films. So she came up with the idea of creating the Ajanta Arts Theatre, a preview theatre where films could be screened and dubbed. Dad went ballistic. He said, "Why do you want a commercial theatre on our property? All these people will be invading our privacy." But Mom

would always find a solution to every problem that Dad would raise. A family friend, the leading architect, I.M. Kadri, was a visionary in his field, and it was he who designed the preview theatre. Mom told Mr Kadri that it was imperative the theatre have an independent entrance. At first, Dad had wanted to use the theatre for his own screenings and asked Mr Kadri to build a tunnel connecting it to the house. Thanks to Mom that particular idea was scrapped and, in 1970, the Ajanta Arts dubbing theatre became the first underground mini-theatre in Bombay, opening the way for many others that followed in the years to come. Mom had great foresight in doing this and, as Dad recalled, "During *Reshma aur Shera*, when we had no other income, the money from the theatre saved us." The theatre was used for trial shows, editing and dubbing. Dad made another rule – we were not to attend any film trials uninvited. Mom, of course, couldn't resist the temptation, and every time there was a trial show, she would go into the preview theatre and see the film, invited or not. She managed to do this thanks to a spy who was posted at the house gate. When the spy would hear, "*Sahib ka gaadi ka horn*" (*Sahib*'s car horn), he came running in to warn her, "*Sahib aa gaye*" (*Sahib* is here).

This charade produced some memorable moments. An adult certificate movie was once being shown, so Mom said we kids weren't allowed. Then she and Shammi aunty went in to watch the film. Suddenly we saw them racing out of the theatre – "*Sahib aa gaye!*" (*Sahib* is here). As it was too exhausting to run up the stairs to the house, they sat down on the steps to catch their breath. When Mom saw Dad coming out of his car, she said, "See, like a devoted wife, I'm sitting here on the steps waiting for you!" It was hilarious. In many ways, she was a prankster – and Sanjay is a lot like her.

Mom's love for books from childhood always stayed with her and in the Pali Hill bungalow she built her own private library, specially designed with wood panels. Her library was so English and filled with books, all hand-picked by her. A particular favourite was Alex Haley's bestseller *Roots* with its memorable hero Kunta Kinte. She spent a lot of time there — writing and reading. When the bungalow was being renovated, we had a librarian who came each week to sort her many thousand books. Mom was an avid reader and would devour an entire book almost every day. She would often read in bed, and when Dad asked her to switch off the light, she would continue reading by flashlight, rather than stop half way through a chapter! Her other passion, shared by Dad, was her love of animals. Dad had a white horse called Daara and rode him every morning on Juhu beach. He had two golden retrievers, Prince and Queeny and, later, Mom had two Pomeranians, Ringo and Silvy. We ended up sharing the house with various dogs, Harry the rabbit, Tipu the white mouse, birds and squirrels. We inherited from Mom and Dad the habit of rescuing stray animals and looking after them. And today our children do the same.

My parents' commitment to family life never wavered. We were given complete support and encouragement in everything we wanted to do — whether it was art in my case, or cinema for Sanjay, or social work for Priya. When I showed a talent for drawing, Mom found a way to encourage me by enrolling me in art classes when I was in the seventh grade. I sat on the floor of the classroom and learnt how to draw and paint. And finally it was Mom who suggested I join Sophia Polytechnic. The only thing that worried Mom was the length of the course — the Commercial Arts course lasted five years — and she said, "*Baap re* (Oh boy!) Anju, how old will you be when you complete this course, and when will you get married?" But it made no difference to her that the course I was following was considered unconventional at the time. She was completely forward-looking and modern in her way of thinking.

As children we weren't interested in seeing our parents' films because we didn't want to share them with anyone. Sanjay disliked the idea his mother was a filmstar and explained, "I couldn't see Mom's films because I was too jealous of anyone else being with her. I still feel the same. So I still haven't been able to see her films. I am still

Above: For a film shoot, Dad rides his favourite horse, Daara.

too possessive about her."

Priya felt the same way about watching Dad's films: "I was so possessive about Dad. If he was in a romantic scene, I couldn't bear to watch. I'd refuse to see the film and shut my eyes and get so upset. It wasn't as if he had done many romantic scenes in his movies! So he told Mom not to bring any of his movies home because of my tantrums. I was always outspoken in front of him. I think I was the only one who would argue with him. But we always had healthy arguments, whereas *Bhaiya* (Sanjay) would say, 'Yes, Dad, yes, Dad,' but would do precisely what he felt like doing.

In our childhood, when we went on an outing or shopping, people would recognize Mom on the street. We usually ignored the chain of whispers that followed her. Her eager fans could be heard saying excitedly as they nudged each other, 'Nargis! It's

Nargis.' When it came to Mom's films, I only saw a few in my childhood. Not until 1991, when I was making a documentary on her, did I watch her films with great attention and learn about her work. In the years when I was growing up, I had no idea she was such a popular and famous actress. My most painful discovery was to think she had been a child artiste, realizing what a difficult life she must have had until she married Dad at 29."

When we were young we knew nothing about cinema. But the film we did see was Dad's *Reshma aur Shera* – Sanjay, who was about 12 at the time, even appeared briefly in the film as a young *qawwal*. It was an Ajanta Arts production and we once went to watch the shooting. Years later when we saw *Reshma aur Shera* again – despite the fact it had flopped badly and Dad had lost a lot of money

because of it – we just loved the film. The colours and the songs were fantastic. It was such a well-made movie with a lot of emotion, and it is so unusual for a film to have so many scenes with no dialogue at all. In our minds, this classic love story was before its time. Probably that's why people didn't really understand the film. It will always be one of our favourites.

Now a star in his own right, Sanjay saw some of Dad's films later in his life and told us: "None of us really knew too much about their movies because we never thought of them as movie stars. Dad was Dad and Mom was Mom. It's weird. Now they're gone, we all want a complete collection of their films, but we really haven't seen much of their work. Among the films Dad produced, directed and acted in, I liked *Reshma aur Shera* and *Mujhe Jeene Do*.

Above: Mom was a huge admirer of Mother Teresa. She admired the work she did for the under-privileged and the dying. Mom regarded Mother Teresa as the most selfless person she had ever met.
Facing page: In 1979, we posed for this photograph, which was sent to our friends as a New Year card. It was impossible for any of these smiling faces to guess that two years later life would turn so bleak.

Among those he only acted in – I liked *Waqt* and *Geeta Mera Naam*. The stories were good and the performances were stellar. *Reshma aur Shera* was a great film. *Yaadein*, the first film Dad produced, acted in and directed was way ahead of its time. It's the only film ever made in India to have only one actor."

In 1980, when Mom was appointed a member of the Rajya Sabha, it changed our lives. It was a hugely prestigious appointment because she was the first actress to be given this honour. Mom had many firsts in her life. She was considered the first lady of

Indian cinema and was the first actress to have been awarded, in 1958, the Padmashree. When she was appointed to the Rajya Sabha (the Upper House of Parliament), she had to commute between Delhi and Bombay whenever Parliament was in session, and we missed her terribly. Her friends in Delhi, including Kusum Sethi, Indira Gidwani, Yog Sharma and Mrs Bawa kept her company.

Priya describes how upset she felt: "When Mom joined politics, it was a big blow because she was no longer going to be home all the time. She wouldn't be waiting for me when I came home from school for lunch. I missed her for other reasons too. For example, I used to be too scared to go and get my exam results. I'd beg her to go instead. I was terrible at knitting and sewing, which we had to do at school, so she used to do the craftwork for me.

Above: We pose for the family album outside Parliament House, New Delhi. These photos show the natural enthusiasm of a family, like any other family, pleased to remember a great occasion with a photo as a keepsake.

Facing page: Mom was the first actress to be appointed as a Rajya Sabha member (1980).

When Mom entered politics I felt I had lost my best friend. Who would I hang out with? So we made a pact. Whenever I'd return home from school and she was in Delhi, she would make sure to call me. Sometimes we went to see her in Delhi, as she had set up a home there. Dad had nothing to do with politics at that stage and was happy for her. He used to laughingly say now Mom had joined politics she could scream and shout at whomsoever she pleases and would no longer need to shout at us."

Her going away was a blow for me as well. In 1980, I was in the third year of the arts course when Mom was nominated a Rajya Sabha MP and we all missed her lively presence. It was during the time when Mom was in Delhi that she began to feel unwell. The first phase of her illness came suddenly and she was diagnosed with jaundice. After that, everything happened so quickly. And no one could have possibly predicted the horrific outcome.

Darkness at Noon

The years between 1979 and 1981 were the most terrible period in our lives. Mom was away a lot in Delhi because of her political commitments. She had been close to Indira Gandhi and when Emergency was declared (between 1975-1977), Mom and Dad stood loyally by Mrs Gandhi, travelling frequently to meet her in Delhi. Sometimes we would go with them. Mom took her duties as a Rajya Sabha member seriously, though we never got used to her being away.

A year before her illness she had started looking unwell. We thought she was overworked and tired because of the incessant travelling between Delhi and Bombay. When we went to London for a holiday, she had some medical tests done, but they showed nothing. She had lost weight; she had aged and had dark rings under her eyes. She used to keep saying she had pins and needles all over her body. Now we know about cancer, we know these can be early symptoms.

In the meanwhile, Sanjay had graduated from Lawrence School, Sanawar. He did pretty well and got admission to Elphinstone College in Bombay. But problems lay ahead for him too. Sanjay explains, "When I got back home, things had really changed. I went to college for a year. It was then where it all

Above: This photograph was taken months before Mom fell seriously ill.
Left: Mom's birthday was celebrated in London in 1980. During her stay there she underwent many medical tests to find out why she had been so unwell.
Facing page: Mom was a close and loyal friend of Mrs Indira Gandhi and when we went to Delhi, we were honoured to meet her there.
Preceding pages 96-97: When Mom became a Rajya Sabha MP in 1980, she was given a house in Delhi. We held a *griha pravesh* ceremony with the whole family.

began. I started taking drugs. I told Dad I didn't want to go to college, but my parents were keen I study further. I never attended college. I told them I wanted to be an actor. Dad said okay and my training started. I learned horse riding, improved my Hindi diction and took acting classes. I realized acting was a tough job. Dad launched me in *Rocky* and I think it was the proudest moment in my mother's life just to see me become an actor."

Sanjay's drug phase was terrible and it added to the intense anxiety of that time. Mom was perceptive, guessing something was wrong with

him. She didn't know what it was and, being a loving, protective mother, didn't believe her son could ever have a drug problem. If anybody suggested he may be on drugs, she'd jump to his defence saying, "My son can never do that. He never drinks and never touches drugs." Sometimes she asked Sanjay directly if it was true, but he knew how to get round her and within minutes she'd forget her question. For a long time, she kept her doubts from Dad who was busy with his films and launching Sanjay in *Rocky*. Not until Mom was really unwell did she share her fears with him.

On one particular visit to Delhi in late 1979, she was suspected of having jaundice and returned to Bombay. She was in such bad shape that she could hardly walk. She had to be rushed to Breach Candy

Hospital that night. Dr Farookh Udwadia detected an obstruction in her pancreas and Dr Praful Desai, a cancer specialist, advised Dad to take her to America as soon as possible, as they didn't have the facilities and equipment to deal with her condition in Bombay. We were told that the obstruction was causing the bile to back up in her system and had caused severe jaundice. If uncontrolled we might lose her.

This was an emergency. Fortunately Murli Deora, who was a close family friend and an MP in Bombay at the time, came to our help. He organized RBI permissions so Dad could take the dollars that were urgently required for treatment and surgery. In those days there were many restrictions on how much foreign exchange was permitted so Murli uncle arranged everything and Dad flew out with Mom the very next day. Our family physician, Dr Puri, accompanied them. Dr Puri remained a close confidante and friend of Dad's, and since then has been by our side in all our times of trouble.

Above (left): Sanjay and Tina Munim in a still from *Rocky*.
Above (right): Sanjay as "Rocky." The film was directed by Dad and made a star of Sanjay. It was largely filmed at Mehboob Studios in Bandra, Mumbai.
Facing page (top): The *mahurat* of Rocky was an important day for the family. (*l to r*) Mrs Mahendroo, Dilip Kumar and Saira Banu (*far right*) joined us for the occasion.
Facing page (bottom): Dad was a strict director. And he could be stubborn too. When Sanjay was late for a shoot in Kashmir, Dad insisted on wrapping for the day. He didn't believe in compromising in work, even when it came to his son.

Dad booked a room at the Waldorf Astoria, but Mom was so weak that he had to carry her inside. While the Waldorf management was arranging a room for them, he sat with her on the hotel steps. He couldn't take her up to her room because she couldn't move. The next day they admitted her to the Memorial Sloan-Kettering Cancer Centre. Unfortunately, they couldn't operate immediately as they weren't able to drain the bile from her system, an essential procedure required before surgery. The operation was delayed for about a month. This delay probably added to the complications that followed,

Dearest Anju,
    Your most affectionate letter - I opened
in flight, but could not read right
through - because I started crying -
I am in such a mental condition,
I have gone far away from all of you,
and I don't what is going to happen,
but I have faith in God, he is not
going to be so cruel as to not
send me back to all of you - I
know how much all of you love
me, keep praying for me that all
will be well with me, Please look
after Sanju - see that he does not get
mixed up with those silly boys again
he is too stupid in his head he
does not realise what he is doing and
how it is going to harm him -
    we are heading towards London,
and from London there is another
7 hour journey - it is very tiring.
As soon as we reach New York

we will talk to you – Give my love to Niki and tell her, her card was really sweet –

I won't forget to bring your Candy shoes, anything else you want, you must let me know after we give you the address –

Lots of love + look after you self and the house –

yours,

MOM.

Left: Mom just before she was diagnosed with cancer.
Facing page and this page: Mom wrote to Namrata on board the Air India flight to New York, just after being diagnosed with cancer. Everyone in the family imagined she would be home within weeks. But it was almost a year before she could return.

as the cancer had started spreading during that time.

While Mom and Dad were in New York, we children were in Bombay. I was in college, Priya was in the ninth grade and Sanjay was busy with his film _Rocky_. We talked to Dad every day, even though making overseas calls in those days was a slow and tedious business. We had to book a call and then wait hours before getting through. The waiting exacerbated our anxiety and tension. The three of us then flew to New York to see her for a few days. Dad told us she'd be back home in a fortnight after the surgery. So we returned to Bombay, reassured. We didn't know it would be almost a year before she could come home.

I remember getting a call from Dad saying the operation was a success. The surgery had taken many hours – they had removed the tumour and the pancreas as well. Dad said, "You can live without a pancreas. She will be fine." That night he celebrated with his friends, including Qazi Moid and Raj Joshi, all of whom, were a great support to him during those difficult times. Then the next day he heard the

1. Feb. 81

My greatest dad-

Dad it was damn sad leaving you I felt like crying but I did not because its a happy occasion that ma is getting better and you all will be coming home soon. Dad please take care of your self eat well and don't neglect your self because now ma is getting better and you cannot afford to fall ill. Dad being in NY for about 3 months I've learnt hell of a lot and these days will never be forgotten, ever- I feel I have grown up in these 3 months they have been very slow and long. Dad please don't worry about us and the house because we are grown up to take care of our selfs you have many other things to worry about - So dad, I say again take care of your self - I'm not so worried about ma because she has many people to take care of her - I'm going to make her room really super. Dad now we have not yet landded in London its 11 pm NY time and I think you must be at the apartment alone but don't worry. you'll be home soon. So take care and give my love

to my ma and tell her to eat well- Give my love to Norma and tell her I already miss her. Give my love to Stella too So I end here dad. and see You soon in Bombay

lots of love + kisses to You and my ma.

love
Anju

AIR-INDIA To my dearest darling maji
I am writing to you on our way
to London. Ma I have told papa
to take you for shopping where
ever and when ever you want
to go. O.K. so don't be disapointed
ma get well soon and come.
home as soon as possible because
we all love you very much and
are waiting for you to come
home. O.K. ma see you ~~bye~~ I love you
very much.
love your own
Priya

To my dearest darling
Pa.
Hi! Papa I have already
starting missing you and mama
very much. but still did not cry as
you had told me. Papa you
have to promise ~~you~~ me that you
will take care of your self and.
eat properly. and bring mama.
hope as soon as possible o.k.
Bye then Papa we a love.
you very much
love
Priya

Top: Young Priya's letter to our parents.
Above: Mom and Priya in 1979.
Facing page: Namrata, who was called "Anju" at home, reassured Dad in her letter that Mom's room would be ready for her return home.

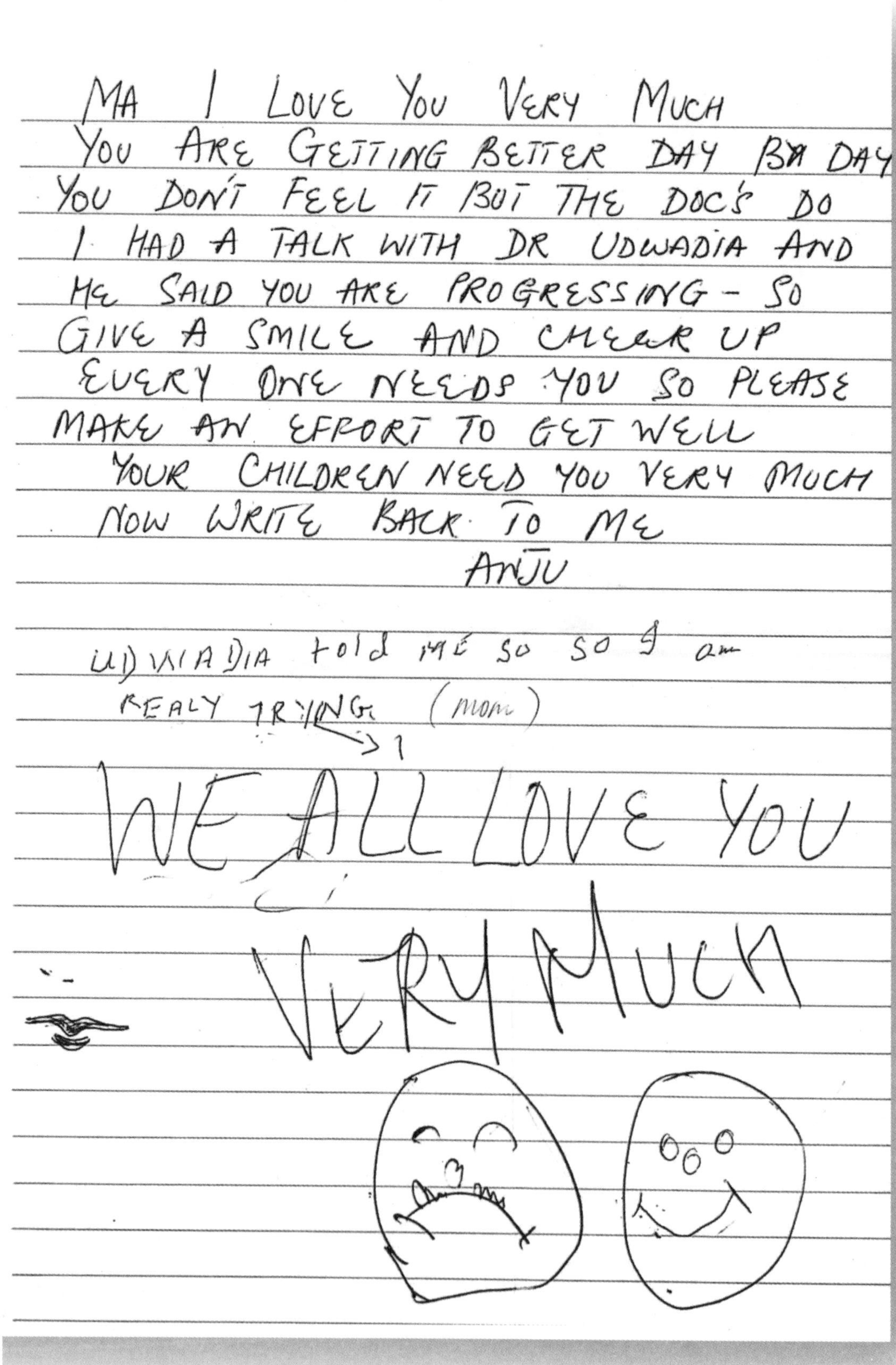

MA I LOVE YOU VERY MUCH
YOU ARE GETTING BETTER DAY BY DAY
YOU DON'T FEEL IT BUT THE DOC'S DO
I HAD A TALK WITH DR UDWADIA AND
HE SAID YOU ARE PROGRESSING - SO
GIVE A SMILE AND CHEER UP
EVERY ONE NEEDS YOU SO PLEASE
MAKE AN EFFORT TO GET WELL
 YOUR CHILDREN NEED YOU VERY MUCH
NOW WRITE BACK TO ME
                    ANJU

UDWADIA told ME SO SO I am
REALY TRYING (mom)

WE ALL LOVE YOU

VERY MUCH

doctors had to rush her back into the operating theatre because she had severe internal bleeding. They opened her up again and tried to stop the haemorrhaging. This happened seven times in two weeks, but the bleeding wouldn't stop. She went into a coma. Her body was in shock. The doctors advised Dad to send for his children. There was still little improvement and she needed yet more surgery. But the doctors refused to operate, saying she might die in the operating room. Dad was in a terrible dilemma. He didn't want to take the decision on his own and said, "I can do nothing without my children." He asked us to come to New York immediately. I remember getting permission from college and Priya's school, saying we had to leave at once and didn't know what to expect.

When we arrived at the hospital, the doctors explained Mom's condition to us, saying, "Don't be too shocked when you see her. She has had multiple operations." They took us to the ICU. This was the first time we were seeing her after our brief visit a few weeks earlier. She was all swollen and her face was completely bloated. She was in a coma, lying there with tubes everywhere. She was on life support for nearly three months.

I remember Mom and Dad had once gone to America on holiday. It was suggested they visit Disneyland, but Mom refused to go without us. Even though she was so keen to see Disneyland, being in many ways a child herself, she didn't. And here we were in America, looking at Mom lying in a hospital bed. It was meant to be a short visit, but the way things turned out, we stayed for almost a year, living in an apartment Dad had rented close to the hospital. We wrote to Priya's school and to my college saying we couldn't come back straight away. Sanju, however, had to return to Bombay because *Rocky* was still incomplete.

It was then we realized for the first time what Dad had been through all alone, how much he must have suffered. Together we took the decision to go

Above: Mom was a firm believer in her guru Swami Muktananda Baba. Our parents often visited him at his *ashram* at Ganeshpuri. Raj Khosla and Bharat Bhushan (*far right*) seen here.
Facing page (top): Mom loved her dogs; a special favourite was Ringo.
Facing page (bottom): (*l to r*) Dad, Nicole Beattie, Dr Praful Desai (the renowned cancer surgeon who first diagnosed Mom), and Dr Edward Beattie (Chief Medical Officer of Sloan-Kettering Memorial Hospital) during a fundraising event for cancer care. The Beatties were of utmost help to us during Mom's treatment in New York, and we regard Mrs Beattie as a godmother.

ahead with the surgery and the doctor asked us to sign some papers. We waited in the hospital during the operation. It was a terrifying time because the doctors had warned us she might die on the operating table. Luckily for us, she pulled through.

The only problem was they couldn't stitch her up because she had undergone seven operations in the same area, and there was nothing left to hold the stitches. So they had to clamp her. During those terribly bleak months when Mom was in a coma, Dad would sit by her side and tell her news of her children, family and friends back home. Although she was in a coma and couldn't react, the doctors told him to carry on talking to her, because she could hear him. We were at the hospital every minute of the day and each day seemed an eternity. Contrary to all expectations, almost three months later, she opened her eyes and finally came out of the coma. Her recovery was slow and painful, and the simple act of shifting position in bed was excruciating as she had painful bedsores. Her

muscles had wasted away because they hadn't been used for three months while she lay unconscious.

Dad told her, "See, the kids are here, they've come from Bombay." And her first reaction was: "What about school? And exams? Have you taken permission from school to come here?" We assured her everything was fine. Characteristically, and despite her fragile condition, she was worried about us more than herself. She had no idea she had been in a coma for so many months. She thought only a few weeks had passed since she had been admitted to hospital.

Mom stayed in the intensive care unit for nine months. Everyone had started calling her "the Miracle Lady of Sloan-Kettering." The doctors said it was medically impossible to survive what she had been through. They also said they had never seen a family like ours and were astonished to see us drop everything and literally live in the hospital ward. The medical team taking care of Mom was really charged up. It became a personal fight for everyone involved. They wanted to do everything they could to help her live.

There were days when she was seriously ill and the doctors would often warn us of the various problems her body was battling, which affected all her vital organs including her heart and liver. Dad prayed constantly. He would recite the *Gayatri* mantra, and go around the building, praying like a *parikrama* for hours on end. Whenever Mom's condition deteriorated, we sisters would go to a little church, right next to the hospital and sit there for seven or eight hours. And gradually we saw her recovering. She slowly started taking a few steps with the help of a walker, but it was extremely uncomfortable. She cried and pleaded with us not to force her to walk because she couldn't tolerate the pain.

It was ultimately her faith in a higher spiritual power that helped her. Mom was a great believer in Baba Muktananda and would take us to his *ashram* in Ganeshpuri, an hour from Bombay. She had always searched for a guru and found one in Baba. For many years, before her illness, she became involved in the *ashram* and had plans to develop it further. Now in Sloan-Kettering, Mom's only thought at this critical juncture was, "If only I could meet Baba or if he could speak to me, I know I'll be all right."

So Dad arranged for Baba, who was fortunately in America at the time, to call her. Baba wasn't too well himself, but Dad requested him to speak to Mom. Baba told her, "Don't worry. Just keep repeating *Om Namah Shivaya*. It will give you strength." We all chanted *Om Namah Shivaya*, and then the whole ICU started chanting *Om Namah Shivaya*, including the doctors, the nurses, everyone. And she started walking, and kept walking.

The ICU was a large oval shape, and the patients' rooms led off the centre where the nurses would sit. Mom used to try to walk all round that oval shape. It was excruciating, but she kept chanting her mantra and walking. The day she managed the full round, everybody – the patients and nurses – came out cheering and clapping. It was so wonderful. Everyone in the ward – someone's Mom, someone's Dad, someone's child – all suffering from cancer, they all came out and clapped. In our shared struggle, we had become like a one big family.

Mom was finally taken out of the ICU to another room where she started physiotherapy. She was feeling stronger. On a small tape-recorder, Dad would record her messages to everyone back home. She sent messages to her brothers, Akhtar and Anwar, nieces Zahida, Rehana and Shahida, and nephew Sarwar, Ameena *nani*, Shammi aunty and all her friends. She was concerned about her dogs, Ringo and Silvy. Ringo had died while Mom was in hospital, but we didn't have the heart to tell her. One day I saw Mom crying and asked her what was wrong. She said she had read a letter a friend of mine sent me with news that Ringo had died. Mom cried herself to sleep that night. She loved her dogs. They were a part of our family.

Priya has never forgotten those unhappy days: "My mother, my Mama ... I was her baby, she cared for me, fed me, bathed me and did everything for me. But during her illness everything changed. Now

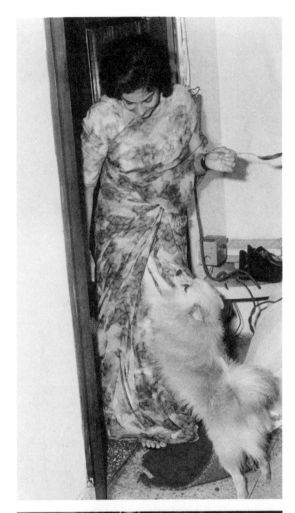

I was looking after her, feeding her, washing her. It was strange how the roles were now reversed. Mom had become like a child. Papa used to sit with her and make her exercise because she had been in a coma for so long, her muscles had atrophied. The doctor said for her to be able to walk, physiotherapy was crucial. So Papa acted like a military sergeant urging her on, 'Come on, Jio, you know you can do it.' As ever, in private, he used to call her Jio. It was a term of endearment she used for him as well."

Mom hadn't seen Sanjay for a long time, so we kept a photo of him next to her bed. When Sanjay had come to New York to see her some months earlier, she was in a coma. His photograph cheered her up no end and she'd look at it and smile. One day Dad planned a surprise. Without telling Mom, he asked Sanjay to join us in New York. It was one of those bad days and she was in a terrible mood and didn't want to eat. Dad said, "Jio, there's someone coming to see you." In an irritated tone, she snapped back, "Now who is it? Who wants to see me?" Then

Sanjay walked in. The expression on her face cannot be described! None of us can ever forget the look of utter bliss on her face. All she then wanted was for Sanjay to sit with her and talk about his movie. She was really looking forward to seeing *Rocky*.

But Mom hadn't forgotten her doubts about his suspected drug habit. She wanted to know if he was misbehaving, or keeping bad company, and if he was all right. He reassured her, "No, Mom, I'm fine." These were the words she wanted to hear, even though Sanjay had probably said them only to make her feel better.

It was her birthday on 1 June. She loved stuffed toys, so we decorated her room with them and hung dozens of birthday cards on strings around the room. She was getting better, but the countless blood transfusions and strong medication had darkened her skin. She had lost all her hair and looked so fragile. Out of the blue, she asked me for a mirror. She hadn't seen her face all this time and, reluctantly, I gave her the mirror. She was deeply upset when she saw her face. Dad came in at that moment and she broke down and cried bitterly. He was so upset with me, but if I hadn't given her the mirror, she would have struggled into the bathroom despite her fragile state and looked at herself anyway. She could be quite stubborn.

Mom still had a lot of determination and will power. When she started walking and felt better, she wanted to go shopping at Bloomingdale's. Dad was encouraging and said, "Let's take her shopping, it will make her happy." The doctor gave us permission to go out, but only for the day. It was freezing. We took her to the apartment first and tried to help her tie a sari. Despite Mom's instructions, Priya and I made a mess of it. She finally couldn't wear the sari comfortably because of the surgery, so we sisters went out and bought her a coat, slacks and a shirt. We teased her saying she looked like a middle-aged American woman in those clothes. She was so conscious of how she looked, how her hair was combed, and whether her lipstick had worn off – she never went anywhere without lipstick. These little things were extremely important to her.

We finally took her to Bloomingdale's. She was so excited to see the store and asked us what we wanted to buy. But she felt tired almost at once and we took her back to the hospital. We were new in America and this was one of the few times we had ventured out. We hardly saw New York and shuffled between our apartment and the hospital, sometimes buying groceries on the way. We knew nothing about cooking, so we used to phone Mom and write down the recipes she dictated. This was how Priya and I learned to cook. Till we had arrived, Dad had survived on coffee and cigarettes.

Christmas Day was another occasion we went out. The patients were assigned a nurse who knew their case history and knew what to do in case of an emergency in the event the doctor wasn't available. Karen was the nurse assigned to Mom, and she became a dear friend to us all. It was she who took us out at Christmas. It was the first time we saw the Rockefeller Center. But Dad insisted we go without him. He never left Mom's side, spending all his time talking to her as she lay in her room.

We had a lot of support from the Indian community in New York. The people we met were warm and generous and became lifelong friends. We shall never forget their love and goodness. Dr Edward Beattie was the Chief Medical Officer and Head of Surgery at the Memorial Sloan-Kettering Cancer Center. Uncle Ted (as we called him) and his wife, Nicole (or Aunty Niki), became extended family and a pillar of strength for us. They helped Dad in every possible way and stood by us through the turmoil we faced then and, unbeknownst to us, would face in the future. Papa also found invaluable friends in Dr Manjit Bains, Dr Jatin Shah, Dr Pahwa, Dr Shashi and Usha Patel, and Qazi Moid. In all those months when Papa lived in New York, they were by his side, giving him emotional support and a greater professional understanding of the disease.

Mom spoke to Dad many times about the plight of people in India who suffer from cancer. She told him, "You can afford to bring your wife to

Above: During the shooting of *Rocky,* Dad took this shot of Mom looking pensive.
Facing page: We joined Dad while he and Sanjay were shooting in Kashmir so that we could have a family holiday.

America for treatment, but what about people back home who can't provide this kind of medical care for their families and their loved ones?" She wanted good medical facilities to be available to the common man in India and longed to do something to make that happen. She desperately wanted to return to her own country. Even though the doctors thought she shouldn't return to India, she insisted. She said, "I'm fine now and I want to go home." The doctors warned catching even a minor infection would be a great setback. But she refused to listen.

Priya and I returned to Bombay before Mom's arrival so we could organize the house. We had to make proper arrangements to ensure that she would be, as far as possible, in an infection-free environment. Her nurse, Karen, was coming back with her to help us look after Mom in the first critical months.

Just before landing in Bombay in February 1981, Mom asked the airhostess to make sure her sari was tied properly. She put on some lipstick and said, "I have to look nice. I'm going back to my country after a long time." Almost a year had passed since she had left Bombay and she was so excited to be coming home.

The Homecoming

The contrasts and similarities in the lives of Mom and Dad were quite pronounced. Dad's life was a constant struggle while Mom faced different kinds of problems. Yet the difficulties in their lives brought them even closer. When Mom came home, her nurse Karen was a great help. Mom had to take insulin injections three times a day and there was a whole procedure to follow. Karen trained us to give Mom the injections and test her sugar levels as well. Mom hated those tiny jabs that ended up turning her fingertips a strange shade of blue. But she had no choice. We did everything to ensure she didn't catch any kind of infection. The doctors at Sloan-Kettering had warned us of the fatal consequences if she happened to catch an infection.

Mom was desperately keen to meet her family and friends. But the return home was both emotional and tragic, as she was confined to the first floor of the house and couldn't meet people freely. All kinds of restrictions were imposed. Everyone had to wear a mask when they went up to see her. Mom kept asking for her dog Silvy. She had found out that Ringo had died when she was in hospital in New York, but we hadn't told her that Silvy had died as well. She would say, "Look at Silvy, she doesn't care that I'm back. She doesn't want to come and see me." We kept making excuses, saying Karen wouldn't allow Silvy to come upstairs for fear of infection. The celebration of her 23rd wedding anniversary on 11 March 1981 was a happy occasion. We dressed Mom up in her green and red wedding sari and a few of her friends came over. She was a little sad that day and said to Dad, "I think this is my last wedding anniversary, Jio." She had tears in her eyes. Dad sat next to her and we looked on in silence.

What made her happy was seeing a few scenes from *Rocky*, Sanjay's debut film. She couldn't sit through the whole film because she was still unwell. Coincidentally, she also saw Kumar Gaurav's first film, *Love Story*. She wanted to see it because Rajendra Kumar (Kumar Gaurav's father) was a friend from the *Mother India* days. Rajendra Kumar had played her son in *Mother India* and she happened to be one of the first people to bless Kumar Gaurav (or Bunty, as he is affectionately known) on the day he was born. Though Mom didn't know it at the time, and neither did any of us, but Bunty and I were destined to marry a few years after Mom died. She took such a keen interest in him that it always made me wonder whether she had some kind of premonition of the future. Bunty remembers when his film, *Love Story*, was released in February 1981; Mom was in Sloan-Kettering and Sanjay called from New York to congratulate him. When Mom came home she told Rajendra Kumar she wanted to see

Above: Despite the traumas of those trying days, Dad tried to contain his emotions.
Facing page: On 11 March 1981, Mom and Dad celebrated their last wedding anniversary. Mom was extremely unwell but dressed in her green and red wedding sari for the occasion.
Preceding page 112: Mom's first outing after months in hospital. She wrapped up warmly and off we set to Bloomingdale's. The shopping expedition was brief and, as ever, she puts on a brave smile for our benefit.

Love Story – and when she did, she showed her appreciation by saying Bunty, was good. She was right. *Love Story* ran for 50 weeks and became one of the most successful films of its time, celebrating a golden jubilee.

Within three months of Mom's return, in April 1981, she tragically caught a urinary infection and had to be rushed to the ICU at Breach Candy Hospital. Karen wasn't encouraged to attend to her needs at the hospital, so reluctantly she returned to America. When I went to see Mom in the ICU, she was sitting on a chair, calmly reading a newspaper. She said "I want to talk to you about something." I

asked, "What?" "I want to see you married." I was 19 at the time and this wasn't a conversation I much enjoyed and quickly said, "Mom, it's a bit too soon." She repeated, "I want to see you married, you're old enough to get married."

Around the middle of April, her situation had deteriorated and she slipped into a coma. The doctors said Mom's respiratory system was packing up and she needed life support. On 2 May, Dad went to Shirdi, a religious shrine near Bombay and returned the same day. We used to take turns sleeping in our van, which was in the parking lot of the hospital and at around 5 in the morning of 3 May, we were told Mom was stable and we could go home, have a shower and return to the hospital later. We were almost ready to leave the house when we got a call telling us to hurry back to the hospital as her condition had suddenly worsened. Dad left for the hospital before us and, by the time we got there, Mom was gone. She was only 52.

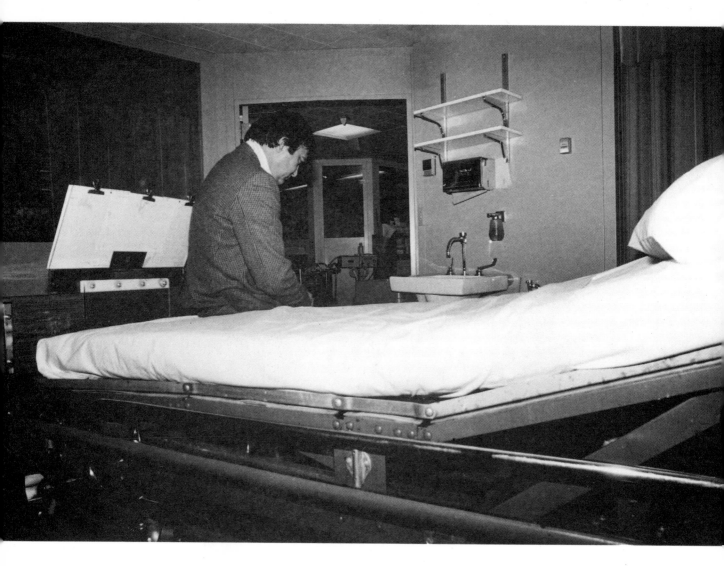

Above: Waiting in the hospital room at the Memorial Sloan-Kettering Cancer Center for Mom to return to her bed. Days turned into weeks and weeks into months as Mom battled against cancer. Dad's friend Jaywant Ulhal took these photographs.
Facing page: We children could never comprehend what it would mean for Dad to lose his "Jio," his "Mrs Dutt." When Mom was no more, Dad took months to return to his former self. We often wondered if he ever fully did.

Priya was 15 at the time and later recollected those last precious moments: "I hadn't realized it was so serious. I thought she had taken a turn for the worse, but it was no big deal. We had survived many a crisis before and she had always pulled through. When I went in, I saw them packing everything. I was about to wear a facemask, and the nurse said, 'You don't need to wear the mask, you can go in and see her.' I still didn't understand. I went in. Dad was sitting there, and so were Namrata and Sanjay. Sanjay looked ashen. Papa was holding Mom's hand. Dad had arrived by her side a minute before the electrocardiogram flat-lined. It was the 3rd of May 1981. It took me a long time to understand how she could die after surviving so much. I guess I was still quite immature. One always feels one has a personal equation with God. You can make Him do things. He had let her survive everything after all. It means she's going to live, nothing will happen to her."

Before Mom's funeral, Dad called the three of us and said we had to be strong and should not cry in front of everyone because many thousands of people would come to offer condolences – there

NARGIS SUNIL DUTT

58 Pali Hill, Bandra, Bombay 50

15 - 4 - 1980.

A WILL

I Mrs. Nargis Sunil Dutt I am writing my will in controll of all my faculties and in complete senses. This is to record: that in eventuality of my passing away anytime anywhere anyhow, I want that all my belongings should be given to my husband Shri Sunil Dutt - My locker should be allowed to be opened by him - he should be in full possession of everything in the locker and deal with the things in them as he likes. My property should be transferred to him, I consider him the only person who can do well with every possession I have - Actually there is nothing that belongs to me, in fact everything is given to me by him. He has been my mentor, my friend, very loving husband, and a wonderful father to my children - I love them all with all my heart and soul. So God be with them at this hour of separation and. I pray for a good life for all of them -

Yrs. Nargis S. Dutt.

Witness

1. (RAJAN RANGA)
   18/4/80.

2. [signature]
   Bombay 18/4/1980

M. K. BATHIJA.
B. A. LL. B.
ADVOCATE,
61 Embassy Centre 4th Floor
207, Nariman Point
BOMBAY-400 021.

would be people who loved her and curious spectators too. He said we mustn't show the whole world the profound grief we were feeling. Mom had explained to Dad the kind of funeral she wanted. She reminded him how scared she was of fire and didn't want to be cremated. He could have ignored her wishes, but he followed her instructions because he had a deep regard for her beliefs and faith.

There were, however, a few arguments. Some Hindus said she had married a Hindu and so everything had to be done according to Hindu rites. Dad said, "No, we respected each other for who we were and her wishes will be followed." He was the one who decided that Mom would be buried in the Bada Sonapur cemetery in Bombay's Marine Lines. She was buried in the same grave as our grandmother, because Mom once expressed a desire to be buried alongside her mother. Dad made the funeral a truly secular ceremony and had priests of all religions there to pray for her.

The other ritual, which created some controversy, was the bathing of her body. A lot of people said we should get a *dai* (nurse), or the older women of the family should bathe her and no one else. Dad refused to let anyone touch her. He bathed her himself with the help of Priya and me and a *dai*. We were young, but it gave us a kind of closure. In those final moments people don't usually leave you alone with your loved ones and this was the only time we were alone with her. We carefully dressed her in her red and green wedding sari. Sanjay couldn't take it – he just blanked out. He was there, but couldn't help with any of the rituals. Until the last minute, Dad couldn't let go either. He loved her so much. Priya and I stayed at home, while Dad and Sanjay took her to her final resting place.

Rocky was scheduled to be released on 8 May 1981 and Mom had told Dad the opening night should not be postponed on account of her and said even if she had to attend the premiere on a stretcher, she'd be there and wouldn't miss it for anything. According to Mom's wishes, *Rocky* was premiered at Ganga cinema hall on 8 May 1981 and we all were there. We sat with an empty seat

Above: Cinema and photography makes people immortal. During those sad moments in May 1981 when Mom was fighting for her life, the images of her would only magnify her absence rather than suggest her presence.
Facing page: In her frail handwriting, Mom wrote her last will, leaving all her worldly possessions to Dad.

between us, kept especially for Mom. What should have been one of the happiest and most important moments for the family, and particularly for Sanjay, became a time filled with deep sorrow and grief. Mom could not witness Sanjay's new start in life after all.

We missed her tremendously. And after her death, I didn't want anyone else to take control of the family. We were so vulnerable and figured someone might take advantage of the situation. I

didn't want that. Mom had been our anchor. She had a career, ran the house, and was active in politics and social work. She looked after three kids and Dad. I knew I had to become like her and, if I wanted to do what she had done, I had to be more organized. I was still at college, but I started looking after Dad and the house. He was so used to her doing everything and for the first few months, he could not accept her loss.

In an interview, Dad talked of those trying times: "For many years after her demise, it seemed as if my hands had been cut off. In many ways, I still feel handicapped." As the eldest daughter of the house, I had to step into her shoes. Dad started

Above: First day, first show tickets for *Rocky* (8 May 1981).
Right: *Rocky* was a huge success and Sanjay became an overnight star. None of this mattered to him when set against the loss of Mom.
Facing page (top): The family visited Mom's grave before the premiere of *Rocky*. (l to r) Aneesa Hussain, Namrata, Dad, Ameena *nani*, cousin Sarwar Hussain and Amarjeet.
Facing page (bottom): Dayanita Singh accompanied us to Rishikesh to perform a ceremony for Mom immediately after she passed away. We immersed the soil from her grave into the Ganges.

expecting me to do everything like Mom and I realized only after she died how utterly dependent he was on her. At the last minute, Dad would bring over friends for dinner and not inform me beforehand. Now all of a sudden I had to organize things and found it difficult. Mom had always been the perfect hostess and could prepare an elaborate meal in no time. This made me wonder how she had managed all those years without complaining.

I used to tease Dad and say, "I don't know how you pack your own bags now Mom that isn't here." If a button on his shirt went missing, he'd get so upset. "Why don't you check my shirts before you pack them?" Everything had to be like, you know, how "she" used to do things. I don't know how he would have managed on his own. He used to ask me to iron his shirts, darn this, do this and that, saying, "I don't want to ask Priya to do anything. She's so clumsy. She'll burn my clothes instead of ironing them." One day he even wanted me to cut his nails and I replied, "Dad, I don't want to cut your nails

today." He retorted, "You want Priya to cut off my fingers instead?" He turned to me for everything – "You do it, you do it." It was a good thing really – it made me much closer to him.

Priya and I gradually took over the running of the house. I had never entered the kitchen before, and now had to take charge. Fortunately we had a cook and staff who lived on the premises, and so the house began to function again. But the ordeal of the past few years caught up with Dad. He was overwhelmed with grief. He was unable to work or sleep. He was falling apart. Nothing made sense to him any longer. He had tried to save Mom, but failed. All the statues and images of gods and goddesses were removed from the house and immersed in the flowing waters of the Arabian Sea. We were angry with God. How could He have done this to us?

The Healing

Dad was devastated. He couldn't sleep in their bedroom any more. We volunteered to sleep in the same room as he did, but he'd wake up in the middle of the night and leave. In a panic, we'd get up and look for him, only to discover he was lying on the sofa in the living room, having fallen asleep again. Sometimes he would go to the cemetery at four in the morning and just sit by Mom's grave. Finally we realized we had to act maturely and be strong for him. He must have felt completely alone. He must have wondered, "What am I going to do with these three children? There's no one to share my life. No one I can talk to." He had shared everything with Mom. His work, his life, everything, and now she had gone.

Priya was just a teenager at the time, but noticed the change in Dad: "He started drinking a lot and smoking heavily. But one day all that stopped. He told me later it was because of something I had said to him. I think every kid has a defence mechanism. You make believe things and it helps. That's how I kept myself going. One day we were standing on the terrace and I said, 'You know, Dad, Mom hasn't left us. You can see her everywhere. Look up at that star, the one that's shining the brightest. That's Mom! She's looking at us. So why are you so depressed when she is with us?' That really got to him. And until this day that star continues to watch over us."

It was during this period Dad realized Sanjay had real problems. And it became a mission for him to get Sanjay to kick his drug habit. After *Rocky*'s release Sanjay had become a star, and with it came adulation and film offers. It was an unhealthy combination in Sanjay's fragile state. But when Dad had made it his purpose in life to get through to his son, he also realized he had to change and practice what he preached. Overnight, Dad stopped smoking and drinking to set us an example.

Finally Sanjay's treatment began. He visited a few rehab centres in India. There weren't too many and they weren't particularly good. He was admitted into a tiny clinic in Bombay. We would take turns to stay with him. Priya had her tenth standard exams, so we'd spend the night with Sanjay at the detox centre, and from there, she'd go and sit for her exams the next morning. Someone had to be with him all the time and Dad was obliged to go back to filming.

Nothing helped Sanjay. So Dad decided to take him to Germany where they stayed with close friends, Jaywant Ulhal, a photographer who worked for *Stern* magazine, and his wife Rajni. They welcomed Sanjay into their home and looked after him during his treatment. That didn't work either. Finally Dad understood no treatment would be effective unless Sanjay himself wanted to pull through. The desire had to come from him alone, and Dad abandoned his mission. One day Sanjay came to him and said, "Dad, I need help. I want to change my life." Until that moment Dad couldn't really do anything.

It wasn't long before Sanjay hit rock bottom and his drug addiction had started affecting his entire life, making it difficult for him to work as well. He no longer had a choice – if he wanted to survive, he had to get help and ask for it. In 1984, Dad took him to America, relying on the help of Aunty Nikkie and Uncle Ted. Sanjay never believed he had a major problem. He thought, "Detox *ho gaya hai*," (The detox is done) and so he could have a drink once in a while. But Uncle Ted and Aunty Nikkie threatened him and said they'd have him deported if he didn't take rehab seriously. It was then that Sanjay agreed to stay at a rehab centre in the outskirts of Jackson, Mississippi. The

centre had trailers in which the addicts lived and the rules were strict. No one was allowed to see him, not even Dad, who was told to go back to India and leave his son behind. They allowed no phone calls either. So we didn't know what was happening – and being a typical Indian family – we were worried sick.

Priya and I were most upset with Dad and bombarded him with accusations: "How could you? You just left Sanjay and came home. You know, you aren't even bothered." Dad went through hell because now he had to deal with three adolescents. Although by then Sanjay was in his early 20s, he still had some growing up to do.

It is never easy for a father to admit his son has a drug problem. Dad saw Sanjay's addiction as an illness and knew his treatment had to be handled by professionals. Dad tried to deal with Sanjay's

Top: When Sanjay was trying to kick his drug habit, he went to Germany for treatment where he stayed with friends Rajni and Jaywant Ulhal.
Above: With Sanjay and Rajni Ulhal during their stay in Germany.
Preceding page 122: Dad was a pillar of strength for Sanjay, and no doubt, in later years, this helped our brother face his own challenges.

recovery in a sophisticated way. There was no undue pressure, but instead a lot of understanding and love. Dad called it "tough love."

Looking back on those dark days, Sanjay recollects: "Anyway, I got out of drugs. I was in treatment for a year in Jackson, Mississippi. It was a

without the dependency on drugs. That's when he realized if people are happy, laughter comes naturally to them. He could be like everyone else. It was a monstrous phase. But incredibly, it was finally over — at least for him. There were 60 addicts at the Jackson centre, 50 managed to go clean, sadly 10 went back.

It was a miracle in a way. It seemed as if Mom had returned from beyond the grave and rescued him. But Sanjay's troubles weren't over. He didn't want to return to India and wanted to start a business in America. After a nine-month stay at rehab, the patients at Jackson were allowed go out into the world alone to find out whether they could stay drug free. Sanjay's counsellor told him, "I have faith in you. I know you won't go overboard."

Sanjay remembered his outing with Bill, his friend at rehab: "Bill took me to Austin, Texas. His father was a big guy in cattle. My God, what a mansion they had! They asked me, 'Why don't you invest money with us? Stay here. We'll raise cattle.' At that time, I had 50 lakhs in India, a lot of money in those days, and I told Dad, 'Somehow or the other transfer the money here.' He asked me why. I said, 'I'm not coming back. That's why.' When Dad came next to America, he pleaded: 'If you respect me, come back for my sake.' He asked me to try and get work in India. But I felt totally cut off. I didn't want to return to the film industry. But I did listen to him and came back to Bombay. I told him, 'I don't want you to launch me again. I'll try to make it on my own. And if I don't get anything within the year, I'll go back to America.'

I swear I didn't try at all. I used to go to the Sea Rock Hotel in Bandra and play squash all day. I was just waiting for the year to be over. One day a producer said to me, 'There's this film I want you to do.' I think acting is in my blood so I asked, 'How much time will it take?' 'Two or three months.' 'Done,' was my reply. I figured the year would be over and the movie completed. I still remember the signing amount — Rs 15,000. I bought some presents for Dad and Namrata and

terrible time for Dad, Namrata and Priya. And for me. I never went back after that, touch-wood. And I have been clean for nearly 25 years. At the centre, I was allowed to make one call a week. I used to phone home and sometimes I'd call Bunty. In rehab we had group therapy where you would talk about different things and get to the core of the problem. My father sent me some audiotapes and they played those tapes during the group therapy session — they were Mom's recorded messages for us during the time she was in hospital in New York. I hadn't known about the tapes. I heard Mom talking to me, saying, 'Be a good man, I want you to be humble.' I started crying and cried continuously for four days. After that everything changed for me because I think till then I hadn't grieved for her when she passed away. So her voice and those tapes changed everything in my life."

Sanjay began to see the world in a different light. He described feeling as if he was a mouse running into a dark room, hiding and doing drugs. And suddenly he saw that life could be beautiful

Priya with that money. The film was called *Jaan ki Baazi*. It was released in 1985 and did well and I never went back."

On his return from Jackson, when Sanjay started acting in films again, he could feel the difference in his performance. He was happy to be drug free. For him being normal once meant doing drugs, and if not, he experienced terrible withdrawal symptoms and was unable to work. When he now sees himself in the films of that period, he admits he looks really "stoned."

Sanjay had won a major battle, not only for himself, but for the whole family. He never hid his addiction. He believed if he could speak openly about his past addiction, it might help others kick the habit. He might become a role model for kids with drug problems. If he could stay drug free, so could they.

After Sanjay returned home, his relationship with Dad dramatically changed for the better. He started taking his own decisions about the movies he would work in, and won more and more acclaim. Dad was so happy with Sanjay's achievements but never told him to his face. Instead he'd tell everyone, "I am so proud of my son." Dad genuinely appreciated the tough battle Sanjay had to fight with his inner demons and emerge stronger. Sometimes victory in a personal battle has greater value than winning a public battle. Dad knew this well.

Sanjay had learned his lessons through experience and was well aware of the kind of support our parents gave him: "I think both Mom and Dad were amazingly great people, so caring. They were also patriotic and really cared for people. The way Mom always tried to help others. She told my father she can afford treatment in America, but what about all those poor people back home who couldn't? She told him he had to do something about it."

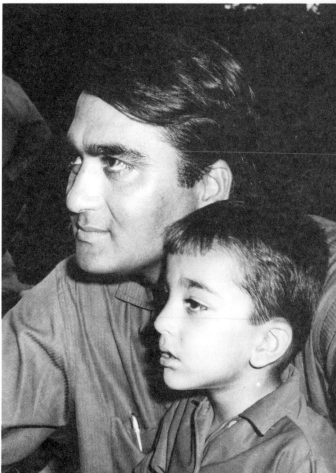

Respecting Mom's wishes and in her memory, Dad started the Nargis Dutt Cancer Foundation. This he did with the help of the Indian community in America and the friends who stood by Mom and Dad throughout their terrible ordeal. The Foundation continues to raise funds and supports projects to improve medical facilities and cancer care in Indian cities and villages. The first chapter of the Nargis Dutt Cancer Foundation opened in 1981 in New York, with branches opening later in various American states. Dad made it a point to go to the US once a year to raise funds. He raised more than five million dollars through fundraising dinners. These funds were used to set up the ICU unit at the Tata Memorial Hospital. He also started the Nargis Dutt mobile hospitals in India, which continue to operate in cities and villages, offering treatment to people who can't get to a hospital. The work he did for the Foundation was close to his heart and he was passionate about it. He knew Mom was right – people in India deserve better health care.

As an actor, director and producer, Dad had already worked in over 70 films, and now wanted a greater purpose and meaning to his life. In 1982, he produced a film about cancer called *Dard ka Rishta* with Smita Patil. The film was no box-office success, but was a sign of the direction he wanted his life to take. All the proceeds from this film went towards the Tata Memorial Hospital.

Dad took Mom's place at the Spastics Society and slowly became drawn to politics through social work. In the process of his own healing, he had found another career. Dad was also actively involved with the People's Health Organization (PHO) founded by Dr Gilada. He became the President of the PHO, which continues to fight against HIV/AIDS, educating people by spreading awareness. He was an active participant in the *Saheli* project, also initiated by Dr Gilada, which focusses on the prevention and control of HIV/AIDS among sex workers. Dad made it a point to visit Bombay's red light areas each year at *Rakshabandhan*. He missed Mom enormously and filled the void by absorbing himself in the work she loved.

Priya and I once found an interesting description of us that Dad recounted in an interview in 1991: "When I see Priya, my younger daughter, I feel she is born of the earth. She is a daughter of the soil in all respects. She is the kind of person who will spend the last ounce of energy fighting for a cause – whether it's something she believes in, or it concerns a friend, or a friend's friend. Money and material comforts have little significance for her. She'll wear anything, eat anything and sleep anywhere. On the other hand, her older sister, Namrata, is just the opposite. She is artistic, aesthetic and fastidious. She does not compromise at all on quality and style. Nothing ordinary is good enough for her and she won't settle for anything but the best in clothes, food and style. And all of this comes naturally and effortlessly to her. It's funny how both my daughters have inherited two completely different aspects of their mother. My wife was the combination of these things. I feel so strange watching them. It's like watching Mrs Dutt neatly fragmented into her two daughters."

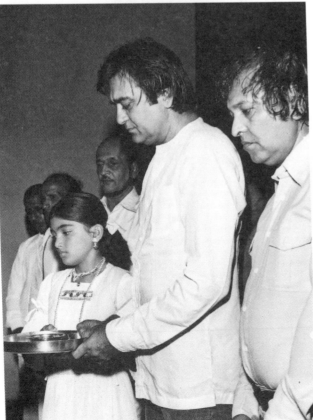

Top: Godmother Nicole Beattie and Rajiv Gandhi attend the premiere of *Dard ka Rishta* in New Delhi, 1982. Music director Ravindra Jain also in picture.
Above: Smita Patil, who starred in *Dard ka Rishta* (1982), accompanied Dad to a special screening, organized to raise funds for cancer care.
Left: Khushboo, Dad and Amarjkeet at the *mahurat* of *Dard ka Rishta*.
Facing page: When Mom passed away, Dad became everything to us sisters. He described us as two facets of Mom.

Above: Farooq Abdullah visits the Spastics Society in Colaba, Mumbai.

Right: The Nargis Dutt Mobile Hospital in Bhuj.

Facing page (top): On January 8 1986 Mother Teresa laid the Spastics Society of India foundation stone on the land that Mom managed to get allotted for them in the Bandra reclamation area in Mumbai.

Facing page (bottom left): Dad giving a moving speech in Mom's memory when he inaugurated the Nargis Dutt Mobile Hospital.

Facing page (bottom right): Dad had tremendous regard for Mother Teresa and felt it an honour to have met her on several occassions.

New Directions

With the many changes taking place in our lives, we discovered a new equation with Dad. The loss of Mom made us intolerant to the idea that he might remarry. We siblings were totally possessive about him, particularly Sanjay. The three of us sat him down and said, "If you ever get remarried, we'll be very upset with you." I actually thought, after Mom's death, there might be another woman in his life, but he never told us about anyone. It was difficult for him because he tried to be both Mom and Dad to us. And it confused him. He could only be Dad. He loved his three children but Priya was his favourite. She was his life. He spent a lot of time with her, maybe because she was the youngest. In 1981, Dad had his first taste of political life when he became Sheriff of Bombay. It allowed him to focus

Above: It was a happy and proud moment when Dad was appointed the Sheriff of Bombay (28 December 1988). Dr Goyal presents the plaque while producer O.P. Ralhan looks on.
Facing page (top): Rajendra Kumar was Dad's close friend and ally.
Facing page (centre): With son and future son-in-law (Kumar Gaurav).
Facing page (bottom): Sanjay and Kumar Gaurav (who is affectionately called "Bunts" by Sanjay) have been friends since childhood. Initially, Sanjay was not happy about Namrata marrying Bunty but soon changed his mind.
Preceding page 132: The Japan Peace March began at Nagasaki on 9 July 1988 and ended in Hiroshima, some weeks later on 6 August.

on the social causes that were close to his heart. Meanwhile, Namrata had found someone next door who was deeply close to her heart. It was Bunty (Kumar Gaurav). Bunty continues to be struck by the coincidence and says: "When I was born, the first person to visit me was my future mother-in-law. She presented me my first set of clothes. It's funny because she wasn't even married in those days and Namrata wasn't even born. She was shooting for *Mother India* at the time. It was the film in which both my father and my father-in-law acted. It was in 1957."

Dad and Bunty's father, Rajendra Kumar, had similar upbringings. Rajendra Kumar was originally from Sialkot (now in Pakistan) and, after Partition, went to Delhi and then finally moved to Bombay. They were both struggling actors and, in the early days when they were trying to get a break in films, Rajendra Kumar, O.P. Ralhan and Dad even shared living quarters for six months. Rajendra Kumar was working as an assistant to producer/director H.S. Rawail while Dad was working at Radio Ceylon. He got his first break in a small role in Kidar Sharma's *Jogan* (1950), which starred Nargis and Dilip Kumar. So Rajendra Kumar had already acted with Mom before Dad had even met her.

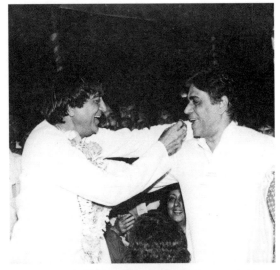

Sanjay and Bunty had become great friends during the release of their respective movies, *Rocky* and *Love Story*. In the eyes of the world, they were professional rivals, but in real life they were best friends and Bunty used to visit our home often. Over time we became friends with Bunty's sisters too. We would all hang out together. When Dad found out about Bunty and me, he summoned him to his office. Bunty was understandably nervous. Dad was clear – there was no question of dating and a long-term engagement. His philosophy was, "If you have made up your minds, better get married at once." Dad arranged to meet Bunty's father the next morning. Rajendra Kumar was waiting for him at his house, on the other side of Pali Hill. They rushed into each other's arms and hugged one another. This was the cementing of a long and valuable friendship. Through the years, they stood by each other through thick and thin. When Rajendra Kumar died on July 12 1999, it was a great loss to our family, and especially to Dad, who fondly called him "High Command".

In December 1984, soon after Dad had given me permission to marry, he became actively involved in politics. Rajiv Gandhi, the then

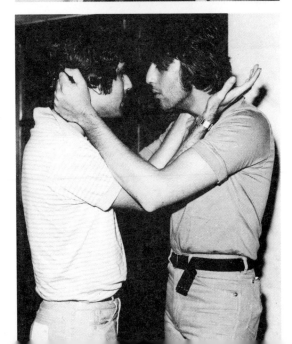

Congress Party President and future Prime Minister, asked Dad to fight Parliamentary elections on a Congress ticket. It was an emotional time. On 31 October 1984, Indira Gandhi was assassinated and her son wanted loyal supporters to join him. Dad's old friend, Murli Deora, helped to further convince him to stand for elections and so he represented Bombay's North West constituency.

With an imminent marriage and an election campaign on hand, the Dutt household was in turmoil once again and I had to make all the arrangements and organize my own wedding. Sanjay was in rehab in America, so I told him about my engagement on the phone. At first, he was quite upset as he thought his friend had betrayed him by falling in love with his sister. When Sanjay was back from rehab, Bunty came over and they hugged and made up. Sanjay was so excited about the wedding and pleased to have Bunty as his brother-in-law. After a long time there was cause for the family to celebrate a happy occasion.

Bunty remembers the joyful chaos that ruled the house: "For most of our wedding preparations, my father-in-law couldn't be around much of the time since he was busy campaigning. It was his first election. The marriage was held on 9 December, 1984 at Namrata's bungalow and the reception at ours. The wedding took place on two ends of Pali Hill. I don't remember who came or what happened – because I was in a daze – I had to ride on horseback from my house to hers, which was down the hill. At one point my *baraat* was left behind and the horse cantered ahead and stopped outside her house. I arrived at her door before the *baraat* could!"

Dad won the elections and by the end of 1984 good times had returned at last. I moved to my new home and Dad became a Member of Parliament. Sanjay's career was doing well and Priya was studying at Sophia College for a B.A. degree in Sociology. Priya remembers those days: "After Mom, *Didi* (Namrata) took care of the home, and when she got married, Dad, Sanjay and I were left on our own. I remember the fights I would have because I didn't want to be answerable to my sister.

Below: Dad performs the wedding rituals. He was so pleased that the Dutts and the Kumars were now one family.
Facing page (top): Dad always placed Mom's portrait in a prominent place at every important family occasion. Guests gathering to celebrate Namrata's marriage to Kumar Gaurav, Mumbai, 9 December 1984.
Facing page (bottom): (*l to r*) Dad, Mrs Rajendra Kumar, Sanjay, Rajendra Kumar, Priya, O.P. Ralhan (Rajendra Kumar's brother-in-law), stand behind Kumar Gaurav and Namrata on their wedding day.

But she was always protective and patient and covered up for me when Dad was mad at me. I understood later what a tough time she must have had creating a peaceful atmosphere at home in Mom's absence. On top of that, she had to deal with Sanjay and me. In the bargain, she had to sacrifice her youth and assume a huge responsibility for someone as young as her. When she left to live in her own home, we realized her worth and missed her tremendously. *Didi* and I became very close after she got married and we are the best of friends today."

Priya was in the last year of Sophia College in 1986. Dad came back from Delhi and announced he

Above: Rajendra Kumar, Sanjay and Priya with Dad as he files his nomination papers for his first elections in 1984. This was a big day for the family as Dad had never previously been involved with politics.

Left: Dad never prepared his speeches, but made it a point to note the names of all the people he had to acknowledge on stage. He could not write Hindi, and like most Punjabis of his generation, knew Urdu, the language he learned as a young boy.

Facing page (above): Raj Kapoor and Dad during his first election campaign.

Facing page (bottom): For Dad's first election campaign, the entire film industry joined forces and organized a massive truck rally. Rajendra Kumar became his unofficial campaign manager. Dad always fought from the north-west district, Mumbai, and, later, Priya was also elected from the same constituency.

Above: Dilip Kumar speaking in support of Dad during his first election campaign. They were forever in each other's company and Dad looked to him for friendship and advice.

Left and facing page: During the years when Dad was involved with politics, he was forever away from home. Though we missed his company, he kept in touch and called us everyday from wherever he was. Also in the picture (facing page) is the character actor Ram Mohan who was a member of the Congress party and remained Dad's supporter throughout his political career.

was going on a *padayatra* (peace march) to Amritsar, starting on 26 January 1987. Sanjay immediately reacted by saying, "Dad, don't do it now." He said this because the situation in Punjab was terribly unsettled at the time. The newspapers were full of horror stories about massacres, terrorism and violence. We all tried to persuade Dad not to go on the march. But he was adamant. Punjab was his homeland, and he felt people had started believing it was a place full of only terrorists. Dad believed someone had to correct that image. He was convinced the people of Punjab needed a healing touch and it was necessary not to alienate them any further. He wanted to promote peace through the

march. We knew he was stubborn and wasn't going to change his mind no matter what we said.

When the day came for him to start his long journey, we went with him to pay our respects at Siddhi Vinayak Temple (yes, we had begun to believe in God again). We also paid our respects at Mani Bhavan, in memory of the original *padayatri*, Mahatma Gandhi. Then we dropped Dad at the national highway. We then went for lunch somewhere. While we were having lunch, Priya said, "I think I'm going with Dad." Sanjay snapped at her, "Now just shut up! Don't irritate me. Dad has just left, and now you're starting." We told her to forget it. But Priya was as stubborn as Dad, if not more.

Priya recalls, "So I called Dad that night and said, 'Papa, I want to come with you.' He simply said, 'If you're going to come, you had better take permission from the college Principal and

everybody.' And so I asked the college for permission. They were most encouraging and said it was an opportunity of a lifetime and I must go. So I called Dad back and he said, 'Priya, I hope you really want to do this and you're not trying to avoid your exams by coming with me, because you'll still have to sit your exams when you get back. There is no turning back either.' I joined him in Bhiwandi and his first comment was, 'The press is here. It will look bad if you back out.' I told him I was sure of my decision and joined him on the march. It changed my life and brought me much closer to him."

Priya was with Dad day and night – it made her really understand him. We had known him as our Dad and husband to Mom, but now she saw him as a person. She saw how he dealt with the world and the different kinds of people who walked alongside him. The *padayatra* was a big learning experience for Priya. Yet Dad never imposed his

views or ideas on her and allowed her to grow as an individual. It was something he always told us, "Whatever you may do, never lose your individuality. You may get married, have kids, but never lose your identity. It's what and who you are." Priya learnt people skills from Dad, as he was so good with people – so patient – always hearing everyone out. He walked exhausted in the hot sun and met lines and lines of people, the young and the old, who were waiting to speak to him. Dad stopped and listened. If he saw anyone pushing the others, he'd tell them not to, saying, "No, don't do that! They've been waiting for hours in the heat." He was fantastic with people.

Our one-year-old daughter Saachi, Bunty and I went to meet Dad and Priya when they reached Indore. Dad missed his first granddaughter terribly and was dying to see her. We were meeting Dad and Priya after weeks. I was extremely upset to see him. He had lost a great deal of weight, had blisters on his feet and his skin was burnt by the sun. Priya was like Florence Nightingale, taking great care of him and the other marchers. The 1987 *padayatra* is vivid in Priya's memory: "Dad was a committed man and left nothing mid-way. During his *padayatra*, he had terrible blisters on his feet, which were extremely painful. There were some Buddhist monks who were walking with us, and thanks to their prayers and their herbal remedies, they made Dad more comfortable through the journey. They would treat his blisters every evening so he was ready for the next day. On the 63rd day, 185 km short of Amritsar, Dad began to feel unwell. He had a high temperature and severe pains in his abdomen. There was a hospital nearby and we rushed him there. He was diagnosed with jaundice. The doctors told me

SPECIAL REPORT: ATROCITIES AGAINST WOMEN

SUNDAY

TRIUMPH OF HOPE

Left: *Sunday* magazine did a cover story following the Punjab Peace March, which started in Mumbai on 26 January 1987 and ended at Amritsar on 13 April 1987.
Facing page: Dad was much loved by his constituency. For him, election campaigning also meant interacting with people from all social classes and communities, which he did with genuine enthusiasm.

he should not continue the *yatra*. I was faced with a terrible dilemma and didn't know how to tell Dad. He would never accept it. We asked Dr Puri to come from Bombay and he arrived immediately. Dad told Dr Puri he wanted to continue walking and requested him to come along, in case anything should happen. Dad said emphatically, 'Don't weaken my spirit. Encourage me to keep walking. Support me if I fall, I will see this journey to the end.' We left the hospital and continued walking. Miraculously, Dad started getting better day by day, and I believe it was only because of his will and determination."

No political party, including the Congress Party directly supported the march. It was entirely Dad's initiative. And many people in his own party

went against him, thinking he was trying to attract attention and gain political advantage. Sometime later when Dad met Rajiv Gandhi, he explained that contrary to what people in politics were saying, he had gone to Punjab to offer a healing touch and not to seek publicity or denigrate anyone.

The *padayatra* gave Priya many insights: "By the time we reached Amritsar, we had received many threatening letters which we code-named 'love letters.' Dad sat us down and asked us if we wanted to follow him into the Golden Temple, since the police had warned us we were risking our lives and might be shot. The police told Dad to wear a bulletproof jacket and he asked, 'How many do you have?' When they said they had only one bullet-proof jacket and it was for him, Dad refused, saying

Above: Many extraordinary days were spent during the Punjab *padayatra*. This was a hugely important experience for Dad on a personal level.
Right: Despite his political affiliations with Rajiv Gandhi, Dad insisted that the Punjab *padayatra* was a personal initiative. Being a Punjabi himself, the communal tensions in the State disturbed Dad greatly and this was his way of doing something.
Facing page: Sanjay joined the *padayatra* in Indore while Priya walked alongside Dad during the long march.

the life of every team member was as precious as his own. When he asked me if I wanted to go into the Golden Temple, I said, 'I am going in. Why else have we walked for 78 days?' 'I respect what you say,' was his reply. We reached the Golden Temple on Baisakhi Day, 13 April. The police sent two plainclothesmen inside the temple with us. The moment we entered, there was a huge crowd of people waiting to welcome us. They recognized the two policemen in plainclothes and told them to go, as they weren't needed. 'Dutt *sahib*'s security is our responsibility,' they said and threw them out."

Before they entered the Golden Temple, the

police informed Dad that they would attack if they heard any gunshots from inside the Golden Temple. Dad was extremely worried and hoped there would be no bloodshed on his account. He wrote his last will, clearly stating if anything should happen to him, he didn't want anyone blamed or held responsible for his death. There should be no anger, no backlash.

Despite the ominous predictions and an atmosphere of fear, Dad and his peace marchers entered the Golden Temple where they had a most amazing reception. Dad was carried on peoples' shoulders with great love and respect. His feet dangled above the ground and, to steady himself, he held onto Priya. There was confusion too. Inside a room, prayers were being recited. Dad pushed Priya into the prayer room. She remembers clearly what followed: "We performed all the rituals in the spirit of devout pilgrims. We met Baba Thakur Singh of the Damdami Taksaal and later five *Singh Sahibaans* or head priests. They vented their anger and hurt. Dad

sat listening to them, as a family member would. We weren't there as outsiders. Not once did we hear Khalistan mentioned or any hint of separatism brought up. In fact, Dad heard the head priest of the Akal Takht going as far as saying, 'Why would we leave India that stretches 3,000 miles from north to south and lock ourselves in 200 square miles?' The important thing for Dad was he wasn't there to negotiate anything, nor was this a political move of any sort. He came with love in his heart and they recognized it. He always believed, 'These boys are like our own children. They have lost their way and alienating them will give rise to more terrorists. They were made into killers by the mistakes of the older generation. We need to make amends. We need to win them over with love.' The media, politicians and everyone laughed at him at the time, but he proved them all wrong when he came out of the Golden Temple alive and a hero. He proved love could conquer."

Challenges

As our life began to settle, a happy occasion was round the corner. Following a whirlwind romance, Sanjay proposed to the young and beautiful Richa Sharma. She was an NRI and an aspiring actress who was introduced by Dev Anand to Hindi cinema in his 1986 film, *Hum Naujawan*. The marriage took place in New York in October 1987 and many close family friends flew over for the wedding. It was great fun being *baraatis*. Sanjay sat on a horse, embarrassed to be riding the streets in full wedding attire with his *pagdi* (turban) on his head. Dad's close friends including George, Uncle Ulhal, Aunty Rajni, Joginder Singh, Naresh Kotak, Qazi Moid, Raj Joshi and many others joined in. Dad made it a point — as he had at my wedding — to keep Mom's photograph next to him. We could

This page: Sanjay married Richa Sharma in October 1987 in New York. As usual Mom's photo is placed in a prominent spot. Sanjay had been through a lot and seeing him married was a big comfort to Dad.
Facing page (top): A typically relaxed moment in the Dutt household.
Facing page (bottom): Dad was very fond of Richa and was delighted to welcome her into our family.
Preceding page 146: Dad was determined to get back on his feet following his stroke in 1999 and promised himself that he would soon abandon the wheelchair. As ever, he kept his word.

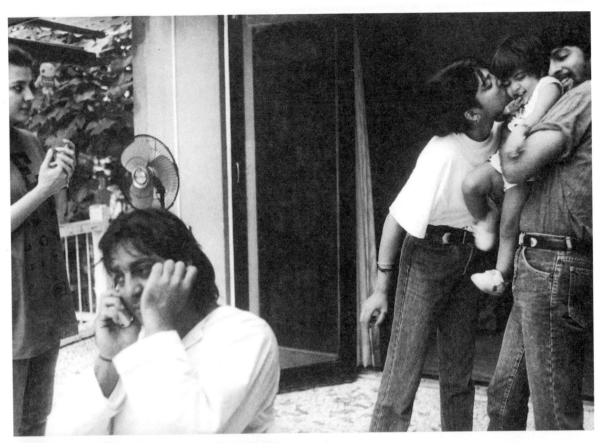

feel her presence during all the rituals.

Sanjay was well settled at last and we all lived together in our bungalow at 58 Pali Hill. Dad went back to his film work, politics and social commitments. He planned another peace march in Japan to commemorate the anniversary of the Hiroshima and Nagasaki atomic bombing. Priya graduated in Sociology from Sophia College and was so excited at the prospect of joining Dad on a march once again.

They left on 6 August 1988, and Priya remembers their new adventure: "We were a diverse group and many old associates from the Punjab *yatra* joined us. There were also many new people who joined us. The *padayatra* had the support of the Buddhist sects Nipponzan Mahyoji and Nichranshu. While we travelled from Hiroshima to Nagasaki, we lived with Japanese families in fishing villages and in temple stupas. We learned about their food, culture and tradition. It was a totally new experience for us. We realized how similar our

Above: Following Indira Gandhi's assassination, it was on Rajiv Gandhi's suggestion that Dad first joined politics. Rajiv Gandhi flagged off the Japan Peace *padayatra* in 1988.

Left: On hearing the tales of the Hiroshima and Nagasaki survivors, Dad breaks down during the Japan *padayatra*.

Facing page (top): The Japan *padayatra* was an easier expedition for Dad and Priya as the Japanese monks who travelled with the marchers healed everyone who fell ill on the way.

Facing page (bottom): Dad too needed the Japanese monks to keep him going. Also seen in the picture (far right) is Bhikhshu Moritaji who accompanied Dad during all his *padayatras*.

cultures and traditions were to theirs. As a country we could learn so much from the Japanese about how they rebuilt their nation following the devastation of Hiroshima and Nagasaki. The effects of that terrible catastrophe are still visible today. The Japanese have made it a point to keep alive the memories of those horrific days and never want people to forget. They want the world to learn from their experience – and to make sure another Hiroshima will never be repeated. At the end of our *yatra*, we heard wonderful news. Sanjay and Richa had a baby daughter and they called her Trishala. It was such a happy moment for Dad, and we celebrated with everyone before flying back home."

Trishala was born in New York on 10 August 1988. After a few months, Richa came back to Mumbai (by now Bombay had reverted to its original name, Mumbai), bringing her baby home. A wonderful year followed, till one day Richa fell dangerously ill. The dark clouds were back again.

Sanjay can never forget those traumatic days: "The shock came suddenly. Within two years of our marriage, Richa complained of headaches, but none of us took them seriously. We'd just had a baby girl – Trishala – and were back in India. When we were visiting Delhi, Richa was feeling slightly unwell and decided to go for a check-up. I couldn't wait for the results because I had to return on work to Mumbai. I was at Delhi airport when my name was announced – I didn't understand why. Then I got a call from the doctor asking me to cancel my flight and come immediately to the clinic. I asked him what the problem was, but he refused to tell me on the phone. So I rushed to the clinic. Richa was lying in the MRI room and the doctor showed me the MRI images. He said, 'She has a brain tumour.' And the whole thing started again, as it had with Mom."

In a reflective moment, Dad said in an interview to a magazine in 1991: "It is strange that all the women I have known have been extremely strong, including my mother, wife, daughters and now my daughter-in-law, Richa. She is an asset to the family and I admire my son for his wonderful choice. But Sanjay and I have had to watch the ones

we love suffer so much. Destiny has chosen us to go through a similar painful experience. Today my grief is frozen and I have come to terms with my life. I was much older when tragedy struck me, but my son is still a child. He doesn't tell me anything, but I know he is suffering. I understand his pain. In silence, we stand united. Without expression, without confessions, we console each other through our actions."

This was such a cruel twist of fate. We reeled from the shock as memories came flooding back. We flew to New York to be with Richa who was admitted to the Memorial Sloan-Kettering Cancer Centre. She was in the same hospital where we had spent nine months with Mom. The same streets, the same little church, the same hospital walls, everything brought back the saddest memories. Richa's treatment began and she fought bravely, with a smile on her face. Due to her unstable condition, Richa's parents thought it preferable she should stay with them in New York during post-

operative care. Sanjay had to return to Mumbai to resume shooting a film he had left incomplete. He had no choice. Richa's treatment continued and she started improving. Sanjay travelled back and forth to see her and their young daughter.

During that time, Priya was studying television production in New York and lived with Richa and her family. She recalls: "Richa's condition was better, but she had bad days and many times had to be rushed to hospital. Trishala was too young to know what was happening. Richa was in and out of hospital. She was one of the strongest women I have ever known. I came to admire her strength and courage."

Richa recovered well following her intensive treatment. The tumour was in remission and she began to lead a normal life. But relations between Sanjay and Richa had deteriorated due to the distance between them. Richa came for a while to Mumbai, but soon returned to New York. It seemed better for her to be near the hospital where

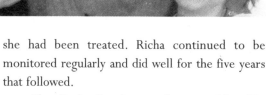

Above and facing page: Dad was a proud grandfather and loved all his grandchildren. After Trishala (facing page) was born in 1988, he went often to New York to see her and Richa.
Top (left): Dad with Namrata's second daughter, Siya.
Top (right): Being the first grandchild, Namrata's daughter, Saachi (born on 6 February 1986), shared a special bond with Dad.
Above (right): Priya with Sanjay and Richa who remained an integral part of our family even after Sanjay and she had seperated.

she had been treated. Richa continued to be monitored regularly and did well for the five years that followed.

Then Dad suffered yet another tragic blow. His leader, Rajiv Gandhi, was assassinated on 21 May 1991. He was devastated to hear of his violent demise. I remember Dad was in Mumbai, out on work, and when I heard the news, I called him immediately. He was deeply shocked. It was because of Rajiv Gandhi that Dad had become active in politics in the first place, and the loss was hard for him to bear.

Dad was an unassuming man and so there were many people who felt he was unfit for politics. He didn't strive to get noticed nor did he do much lobbying for himself. He was never pushy in the

Above: Dad offers a prayer for Rajiv Gandhi.

company of Party leaders and colleagues, but when necessary, he asserted himself. Dad was a loyalist and spoke his mind without being in your face. This is why he earned everyone's respect. Senior leaders, not only in his own Party, but in the opposition Parties thought well of him too. After the Prime Minister's demise, Dad continued to work hard for the Congress Party and pledged his support to Rajiv Gandhi's family in their time of grief and sorrow.

Dad threw himself into work, continuing his *padayatras* and peace initiatives. His friend Akhil Bakshi, the great explorer, organized expeditions that were hugely attractive to Dad, as the idea of a new adventure never lost its appeal. In 1995, he joined the Azad Hind Expedition, which meant travelling in a convoy of jeeps starting from Singapore, and covering a distance of 10,000 miles. They journeyed through Malaysia, Myanmar, the North-Eastern states of India, West Bengal, Bihar, and arriving finally in New Delhi. The idea behind the expedition was to bring attention to the

sacrifices of Subhash Chandra Bose and the INA, and Dad had for company two original INA members Colonel Dhillon and Captain Laxmi Sehgal.

Dad was also interested in promoting communal harmony and even before the Babri Masjid had been demolished, he walked from Faizabad to Ayodhya in Uttar Pradesh, talking to people about peace along the way. He always told us he had not met a single person who felt the Babri Masjid should have been destroyed — they all said how sad they were to see its destruction.

Dad never discussed any problems he may have had in his political life at home. It was only when something major happened in the country that he'd discuss it with us. The friend whom he greatly respected and whose opinion and advice he always sought was Dilip Kumar. Every time Dad would feel low and confused, especially about things concerning his political work, he'd walk across to

Dilip uncle and Saira aunty's house and spend hours chatting with Dilip uncle. Many times he'd say, "I'm going to have lunch today with Dilip *saab*." Dad loved the food made in their home – they were Dilip *saab*'s own recipes and he thoroughly enjoyed these shared meals.

Another way Dad had of unwinding was cooking. He found it therapeutic and believed he was literally stirring away his problems. He loved feeding us, always claiming food tasted better when made with love, not out of obligation. Dad's famous recipes included prawn pasta, stuffed roast chicken (this recipe he credited to my daughter Siya, saying it was she who had told him what to add in order to create the dish), and *matka gosht*, mutton cooked in an earthen pot. He would invite all his friends over for his *matka gosht*, and an entire ceremony had to take place before we were allowed to open the earthen pot to relish the fabulous meal. When he travelled to America to fundraise, many friends told us how he would cook for them. He often told Priya someday he would write a recipe book.

Priya remembers spending time with Dad in the kitchen: "Our cook Chottu went on leave for a month every year and Dad took it on himself to cook us a meal each day. He would tell me, 'Please don't cook because you don't put your heart in it!' By the time he returned home in the evenings, the daytime staff had left, and there would be only Dad and me in the kitchen. He would put on an apron, open a bottle of wine and pour himself a glass. Then he was ready to start cooking. I washed and chopped the vegetables and he would do the rest. We had a great time. After the meal was done, Dad helped me clear up and then I washed the dishes."

At home our life was simple. It was sometimes his professional life that was complicated, especially when he chose to swim against the tide. But he could never have foreseen the greatest blow that was in store for us. And, unbelievably, it was Dad's desire for communal harmony, which led to it.

Following the demolition of the Babri Masjid, there was rioting in Mumbai in December 1992 and then again in January 1993. There were reports of violent incidents everywhere. Our cousin who lived on Carter Road, in Bandra, left his home fearing an attack, entrusting his young daughter, Sanam, with us. As we were involved with relief work, our house had been turned into a kind of relief centre, and trucks laden with donated supplies and food grains arrived at home. We repacked the supplies, which included food and medicine, and sent them to people in need.

Priya remembers that frightening and uneasy time: "Papa, Sanju and I would fill trucks with food and medicine, and drive to the slum areas. People claimed Dad was only helping Muslims; and so gave his work a communal slant. But it wasn't true. Then Papa had to go to Delhi, and there was only Sanju, my niece Sanam, and me at home. That's when we started getting threatening phone calls. The situation got worse by the hour. Then one day Dilip uncle and Saira aunty called and told me, 'Priya, we have news that both our homes are going to be attacked. Why don't you come over here now?' I explained I couldn't leave the house empty. It was very scary and unless you are faced with a similar situation, and overwhelmed by the fear it evokes, you can never second-guess how it feels. People were calling us in a panic saying, '*Voh hamein maarne aa rahe hain, hamare bachchon ko ghar se nikaal rahe hain* (They're coming to kill us. They're dragging our children out of the house).' We were overcome by a sense of helplessness. All we could do was telephone the local police station and tell them about the calls we were receiving from various neighbourhoods, begging for help. We insisted the police look into the situation urgently. In the days that followed we kept hearing horrific stories about people being massacred."

In January 1993, Dad resigned from the Lok Sabha in protest that the Government wasn't doing enough. Given the terrible situation in Mumbai, he felt that the Army should have been deployed sooner, and doing so would have saved many lives. Alas it didn't happen and Mumbai burned for days before the Army imposed curfew. The situation was

① Buy chicken.

② Cut the chicken from the Stomach.

③ = Put glass of stuff
Salad inside the
Stomach of chicken.
Salad green
olive oil
close the stomach.

④ outside & inside
the stomach put
chilli +

⑤ Take Hot water.
Cook for Two
Minutes -
& then it is made.

⑥ Get oval Type
plate - place the
chicken on it -
make some chicken
gravey - put on
the chicken & then
put gravey & chicken
on the oval plate -

⑦ and then
put all Sorts of
Vegetables around
the chicken - put
olive oil on
the Vegetables -

going from bad to worse. Instead of Dad's resignation acting as pressure on the Government to do something, it boomeranged on us.

Then, following the devastating riots, another devastation was about to happen. On 12 March 1993, Mumbai was hit by a series of bomb blasts creating terror and havoc in the city. Those days are still vivid in Priya's memory: "When the bomb blasts happened in March, I clearly remember I was in Jaipur with Sanjay, who was filming there. We heard there were a series of blasts in the city. We were utterly shocked. Sanjay left for a shoot in Mauritius shortly after that. Then suddenly, out of the blue, articles started appearing in the press talking about illegal weapons being found in different parts of Mumbai. And Sanjay's name popped up in the papers as being someone who allegedly possessed a gun."

Dad got extremely worried and wondered what was going on. He met with many people in high places and told them, "My son is in Mauritius. Since there is nothing to hide, I'll call him back right away if you want." He was advised to ask Sanjay to return so the police could record a statement. Dad was reassured there was nothing to worry about. He called Sanjay in Mauritius and told him to come back, saying not to worry, and all the police needed was to clarify matters and record a statement. On 18 April 1993, Bunty, Priya and I went to the airport to receive Sanjay. Suddenly we noticed there were policemen all over the place. The airport had been cordoned off. While Bunty was allowed into the Customs hall, we stood around wondering which VIP was going to arrive. We later discovered they had come for Sanjay and arrested him in the aircraft as soon as it landed.

We were terribly upset when Bunty told us what had happened to Sanjay, and we rushed home and told Dad, "They have taken him away. We couldn't talk to him or even see him." Dad was flabbergasted. When Bunty called again from the Crime Branch at Crawford Market, we told him not to leave Sanjay's side. So Sanjay and Bunty sat there together, all night long. The police didn't talk to

Above: Come rain or shine, Dad would be out there talking to people throughout the country.
Facing page: Mom learned to cook after she was married. Dad was, however, a passionate cook and loved making lavish meals. His recipes weren't famous for their precision, but in his hands the results were finger-licking good.
Facing page (bottom right): Dad loved cooking for his friends and here he prepares a meal for Kuldeep Vaid (President of the Nargis Dutt Cancer Foundation, Portland chapter) and his family who live in the US.

Sanjay or ask him anything. Sanjay and Bunty were puzzled and didn't know what was going on. In the morning, the interrogation began. One thing led to another and the situation got worse and worse. We realized Sanjay wasn't coming home in a hurry. Dad then ran from pillar to post, trying to understand how this worrying situation might be resolved. This was the first time we saw Dad in such a state. He was overwhelmed with guilt, thinking if he hadn't resigned or protested publicly, this would not have happened. After they arrested Sanjay, everything went wrong.

Until that point in time, our family held a kind of a record in as much as we never had an income tax raid, a frequent occurrence in the lives of movie stars. And now a warrant had been issued to search our home. Dad was away and we sisters were at the bungalow along with Bunty and his father Rajendra Kumar. A battalion of policemen arrived with search dogs. It was a deeply humiliating experience. In Dad's absence, Rajendra Kumar took over and told the police: "I'll open everything. Tell me what you want." We watched as they combed every room, every cupboard. Nothing was found.

In the days that followed, Dad kept trying to get Sanjay released from prison. He met every possible person who could help to explain the legalities involved. We were so unaware of what was needed to be done, as none of us had any previous dealings with the law. Through the High Court, Dad managed to get Sanjay out on interim bail on 5 May 1993, and Sanjay came home. We were so happy and relieved to have him back. We all knew he would have to face a long legal battle ahead, but having him home was a great comfort. A few weeks later, at dinner with friends, Sanjay met Rhea Pillai and they soon got emotionally involved. By this point in time Richa (who lived with Trishala in New York) and Sanjay had grown far apart. Yet they remained close friends and Richa knew she could count on him.

In July 1994, when the charge sheet had been filed, Sanjay was re-arrested. Rhea visited him frequently in prison and did whatever she could to be there for him. Sanjay is highly emotional about that time: "I was accused of being anti-national and a terrorist. What a terrible blow to my family. I hated Dad seeing me in such conditions, knowing how it used to kill him. I constantly asked, 'When am I coming out?' One day when Dad came to meet me, he held me by my shoulders and said, 'I can't do anything.' As he spoke he had tears in his eyes. I was shattered because I thought Dad was my only hope. And once I saw that hope evaporate, I gave up, and reconciled to the new reality. Inside the prison it was crushing to look outside and see people walking about free. The cell was small. I shared it with someone. I slept on the floor and read a lot. I couldn't exercise because I wasn't in the right frame of mind to do anything. I read the *Gita* and the *Ramayana*. I also read Mandela's book, which really inspired me."

Both Mom and Dad had always worked for the country through the years. They were committed patriots and the love they had for their homeland was reflected in their actions. But now our family had been branded anti-national. Dad was a broken man. This was the first time we saw such helplessness in his eyes. A man who was a pillar of strength to us seemed to be collapsing. On top of that, we had many financial problems, we had no money coming in and the legal expenses were mounting. People suggested all kinds of solutions, even spiritual ones. In his worried state, Dad didn't want to leave a single stone unturned. He was told the Pali Hill bungalow was unlucky for Sanjay – and to lessen Dad's financial pressures – he should consider demolishing it and building a new highrise in its place. Dad finally decided that we should move out and we shifted to Apsara, a building down the road from our bungalow at 58 Pali Hill. We were overwhelmed with sadness at leaving our cherished home with its rooms so filled with happy memories of growing up with Mom and Dad. This was when Sanjay took a stand and the next time Dad visited him in prison, he said, "You are not alone. We will face this together."

Dad became obsessed with Sanjay's situation and his behaviour became increasingly erratic. He was beside himself. He didn't sleep and would get up at four in the morning and say, "How can I sleep when I know my son is in the same city, a few miles away from me, lying on a cold stone floor?" Dad didn't eat either. While Sanjay was in prison, we had some support at first, and then slowly people

Top: The two-rupee coupons that Sanjay gave us when we visited him in prison on *Rakshabandhan* remind us of the complexity of life and, above all, the importance of emotional bonds.
Facing page: Letter dated 29 October 1994 to Priya from Sanjay. This was written when he was at Thane jail.

Where is photograph?
Baba's photograph.
Anyone is sending.
Send it soon.

Thane Jail 29th Oct. 94.

My dearest darling Sister Pri
Hi! I hope you all are
fine, and I hope you all have got my
speed post. The days are passing slow
and it get boring in here, but I have
to pass them somehow — I read, write
and pray a lot. I started reading the
"Ramayan" today and it is fantastic.
I really, haven't seen you properly nor have
I received any letters from you — please
write back to me and tell me whats
happening. Its 11.30 at night right now
and I can't sleep, I am thinking about
all the Diwali's we all spent together
and it makes me sad that I can't be
with you all this year, but God willing
and with the grace of Baba we will
have many more beautiful Diwali's together.
Pri this Diwali call Rhea home and let
her spend Diwali with the family - it
will make me real happy.

You know Pri today I washed my
room — I put water and those Dettol
soap took a Jhadoo and really did
सफाई like we used to do on our terrace
and now my room is all shining. Dad
came to see me today and he was sounding
pretty good and positive and that was good.
I wonder what's happening. He keeps telling
me November things will fall in place —
I hope it is TRUE— I am dying to come
back home now, its enough. How is Anj
Saachi and Siya? tell them I miss them
and how is Bunts? tell him to have a
drink one for me. Rest all is fine I
just hope to be out soon — at least
by Dec end or early Jan. I pray to
God to make that possible. I miss you all
and love you all too much. Write and
tell me what's happening anything positive
Rest all fine — I love you and miss you
too much. Lots of love
Your Bhaiya

started drifting away. We were on our own till help came to us from an unlikely quarter. Mr Bala Saheb Thackeray made a public declaration saying he didn't believe any member of the Dutt family could be anti-national. He had a high regard for Mom and Dad, and his statement made a huge difference in public perception. Dad and Sanjay were so grateful for his support, which came at a time when it was needed the most.

On *Rakshabandhan*, Dad took special permission for us to visit Sanjay at the Thane Central Prison where he was incarcerated. Dad, Priya and I waited in a private cabin. When Sanjay was brought in, we were so happy to see him, to be able to hold and hug him after so long. Our eyes soon filled with tears. Dad calmed us down saying, "Tie your *rakhis* and give him strength." We had taken *thalis* with us and tied a *rakhi* on his wrist. Sanjay looked sad and said, "I have nothing to give you both, but I've saved these coupons for you. This is all I have." He gave us the coupons with which you can buy tea and snacks in prison. He had saved those Rs 2 coupons for us, and we still have them. It was an extremely emotional moment. It was the first time we saw Dad break down and cry. When Mom passed away we knew his despair, but he refused to shed a tear in front of us. We locked each other in a long embrace and wept, unburdening our hearts, before Sanjay was led back to his cell.

My younger daughter Siya was only two and my eldest daughter, Saachi, was seven. They kept wanting to meet their Sanju *mama* (uncle). I believed they had to be told, as the other kids in their school were talking about the case. We explained everything to them and took them to meet him in prison. Sanjay sat behind the prison bars and the two little girls sat on the other side. It took Siya a long time to understand what had happened to her uncle. She was so traumatized that she couldn't speak to Sanjay for nearly 10 years. Only recently has she started talking to him again.

It was difficult to bear the humiliation we faced every single day. Our lives had been so sheltered. We sisters had never seen the inside of a

police station and here we were outside a prison, waiting in line to see our brother through barred windows. Being asked to taste the food we took for him, or searched as though we were criminals was something that was never part of our reality. But we saw so many other families facing this trying situation, and realized just how lucky we were to afford good lawyers for Sanjay and have a father like Dad.

Sanjay was granted bail by the Supreme Court in 18 October 1995 after 16 long months in prison. The court order came and once the paper work was done, he was released. Outside the Arthur Road Prison, thousands waited to see him. We took him to Siddhi Vinayak Temple, and to a *dargah* and church in Mahim. Then we brought him home. It took Sanjay a while to adjust. He couldn't sleep at night, and was depressed and withdrawn. He refused to be alone and when he went to bed at nights, he left on the light. Then one day we heard Richa was in hospital again. The tumour was back, and this time it was more aggressive.

Priya was in New York at the time: "I remember going to visit Richa in hospital and realized something about her had changed. She seemed to have lost her will power. She wasn't fighting the way she had the first time round. The doctors said she would slowly lose all her senses. When I went to see her, she didn't seem to respond to anyone. Then we saw what no one expected to see. Sanjay rushed to New York to be with her, and the moment she saw him, she had a smile on her face and a sparkle in her eye. We were stunned since she hadn't reacted to anyone like this. Richa truly loved Sanjay right to the end. On 10 December 1996, she died as Mrs Dutt, with pride and dignity."

It was particularly tragic for Sanjay and Dad to lose their wives in similar circumstances. They relived the horror and the feeling of helplessness for

Above: Dad and Priya during the "Hands Across the Borders" expedition (March 1999), organized by Akhil Bakshi. They started from Bhutan and travelled to Bangladesh and Sri Lanka.

Right: Dad riding a rickshaw with a Bangladeshi delegate as passenger.

Facing page: The family celebrating Dad's sixty-seventh birthday. *(l to r)* Namrata, Saachi, Siya, Bunty, Sanjay, Dad and Rhea. During the days when Sanjay was first in prison, Rhea was a tremendous support to him, visiting him whenever it was possible.

a long time. Despite the emotional wrench of living apart from Trishala (she lives with her grandparents in New York), Sanjay believes it was the right decision and is proud to know that she will soon become a lawyer. For Sanjay there is a close and strong bond between him and his daughter. He knows the whole family feels the same: "Dad had a great relationship with Richa and Trishala. He absolutely adored them. Trishala is particularly close to her cousins, Saachi and Siya. She visits us in India and we travel to the US to be with her and Richa's family."

Sanjay moved in with Rhea and on Valentine's Day in 1997, they were married in a rushed and quiet ceremony. Their marriage took us all by surprise, but we were happy for Sanjay. He deserved some stability in his life and we hoped his relationship with Rhea would provide it. In the years that followed, Sanjay worked in many films, rebuilding his career. Our lives had been on hold too, and gradually a sense of routine and normality returned to the home.

In the meantime, Dad was persuaded to go back into politics. His respect for the Gandhi family

tilted the balance and, in 1999, he stood for elections again and won. With Akhil Bakshi, Dad prepared a trip to the SAARC countries in an expedition called "Hands Across the Borders." The peace expedition included journeying through Sri Lanka, Bangladesh, Bhutan, Nepal and various parts of India. Priya joined Dad at the Bhutan border and drove with him in his jeep through Bhutan. Dad's passion was travel and adventure. He worked round the clock and hardly ever took a break. We often complained that we never went on holidays as a family. To which he would say, "You're grown up now and have your own families."

Priya was nearly always at Dad's side and was aware that her being unmarried concerned him: "Dad was worried about me. He always encouraged me to stand on my own two feet. He used to say, 'Once I am gone, there will be no one to take care of you. So you had better learn to be independent and strong.' I loved spending time with him because I felt I was sharing his adventures. Thanks to him, I had the opportunity of experiencing things I couldn't have otherwise. It would have taken me a lifetime to learn what I did by his side. He was

Above: Dad and his camera were inseparable.
Above (right): On holiday in the Maldives, December 1999.
Facing page (top): Dad's holidays in the Black Forest in Germany were his only escape from relentless responsibilities.
Facing page (centre): Enjoying a glass of wine with friends in Germany.
Facing page (bottom): He enjoyed all kind of sports, including snorkelling. Maldives, 1999.

my Peter Pan, and I flew behind him from one adventure to another. And yet Dad never failed to give me the freedom and space to enjoy my own experiences."

Usually in October and November, Dad travelled abroad. He dedicated this time to the Nargis Dutt Cancer Foundation, touring America and Canada to fundraise. He had amazing stamina and his travel schedule was hectic. The rare time he took a break was when visiting friends in Germany, in the company of Jaywant Ulhal, his wife Aunty Rajni, Uncle Joginder and Uncle Mohanty. Together they would plan every detail and usually follow the same itinerary, involving a drive to the Black Forest and staying in a quaint village hotel owned by a German couple. They went on long walks in the woods, enjoying a glass of wine in the evenings and relishing good food. They explored the area around the Black Forest and visited nearby sites. He loved it there. Every time Dad returned home, he looked

younger and fitter, promising the whole family a trip to the Black Forest before long.

When Dad returned from a fundraising trip to America in 1999, he was feeling unwell. He had a high temperature and complained of pain. Dr Puri came to see him and gave him some medicine. The next day Dad asked Priya to take him to the hospital as he was in great pain. Priya immediately called Dr Puri who arranged Dad's admission into Lilavati Hospital in Bandra. The area around Dad's neck had become extremely painful. Dad ascribed the pain to a minor car accident he had during the "Hands Across the Borders" expedition. While driving through Nepal, his head had smashed into the jeep's windscreen. The impact shattered the windscreen, but he wasn't considered badly injured, only suffering a sprained neck. It seemed unimportant at the time and no one really gave it much thought. On 22 November 1999, we were asked to go to Breach Candy Hospital in South Bombay to have an MRI done. During the MRI, Dad was unable to lie still and cried out in pain. None of the painkillers seemed to work, and so later he was made to lie down in a private room.

Priya remembers that day very clearly: "Dad told me that his legs were feeling numb. I reassured him, saying it was probably the hospital room that was too cold. He asked me to rub his legs. A few minutes later, Dad said, 'Priya, I told you to massage my legs.' When I explained I was doing just that, he reacted by saying, 'I can't feel a thing.' I tried to raise his legs and he told me he felt no sensation at all. I called the doctor at once and luckily Dr Udwadia was at the hospital and immediately administered high doses of steroids to arrest the paralysis."

The stroke was progressive and had started from his feet working its way up. Mercifully, the doctors managed to arrest it at his waist, halfway through his body. If it had gone any further, it would have completely paralyzed him, and affected his heart and lungs. He would have needed life support to survive. This was the biggest blow imaginable. Dad was always there for us, through thick and thin, and here he was in this critical state. Sanjay and I went immediately to see him. Sanjay was totally disoriented with shock and I broke down in tears. I couldn't bear seeing Dad lying in bed unable to move. We asked Dr Udwadia how quickly he would recover. The doctor said he couldn't say if Dad would recover at all. He said he might never walk again.

The doctors were puzzled by Dad's sudden paralysis. They could only link it to the minor car accident in Nepal. So once again we called our friends in America for medical advice. Now it was Dad's turn to lie in a hospital bed. He had a smile on his face and confidently said everything would be all right. But we knew there was a strong chance he would never walk again. The doctors then moved him to the ICU. Dad was determined he would walk out of the hospital and didn't care what the doctors said.

From that day on, until he was ready for physiotherapy, Dad did everything in his power to speed up his recovery. But he could only manage small movements on his own, like wiggling his toes. And that's what he did in his hospital bed; wiggle his toes all day long. His physiotherapist, Dr Sujata Wagle, was a great help. She was so moved by his grit and determination that she worked extra hard to get him back on his feet.

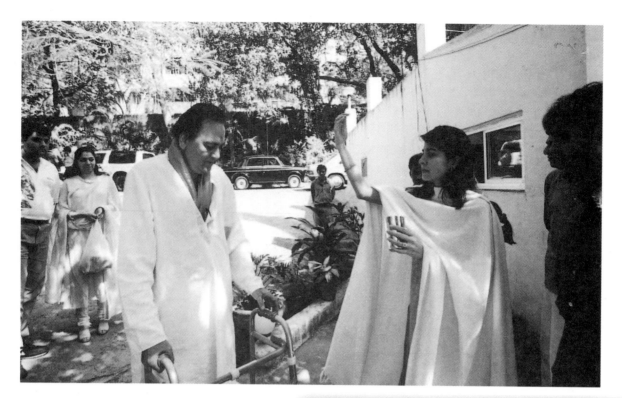

On 18 January 2000, the day had come at last when he did walk out of the hospital. That was a day of triumph, not only for Dad, but for everyone who helped make him get well again, including the doctors, nurses, ward boys, the entire staff of Breach Candy Hospital and, above all, his physiotherapists. On the day he was leaving the hospital, he refused to use a wheelchair. The doctors insisted, saying it was hospital rules. So he sat in a wheelchair until he reached the exit on the ground floor. Then he got out of the wheelchair and with the help of a walker and with a huge smile on his face, he made his way out on his own two feet. Everyone looked on with amazement and tears in their eyes.

In the months that followed, Dad was obliged to wear a neck brace and continue physiotherapy at home. This he did thanks to Sujata Wagle, his therapist. His sense of balance wasn't very good so we built bars all around the house so he could support himself when he walked. Dad was deeply attached to Prince, our Golden Retriever and Prince was deeply attached to Dad. When Dad was in hospital, he missed his favourite dog and told

Top: Following his plane crash, Dad found he had to use a walker all over again. After months of physiotherapy, he was back on his feet. Like Mom, he had the spirit of a fighter.
Above: Even when he was in hospital, Dad asked us to sneak in our retriever, Prince, so that Dad could see him.
Facing page: The plane which crash landed near Nashik with Dad and Mukesh Patel's family on board.

Priya, "When I go down in the morning for physio, bring Prince to the hospital or he'll forget me." When Dad returned home, Prince never left his side and whenever Dad practiced walking around the house, the Golden Retriever would lay down right in the middle of his path. Dad used to say, "He's doing it only to help me, so I can learn to manoeuvre round any obstacle and improve my balance." Dad was confined to the house, but he pushed himself hard and slowly got stronger. And though needed a walking stick, he was back on his feet again and finally returned to Parliament on 21 November 2000, a year after his stroke. During all that time, Priya never left his side.

To make matters more complicated, Dad met with another accident. He had gone to attend a function in Shirpur organized by Mukesh Patel, a close friend. On the return flight, the pilot lost control of the small aircraft Dad and Mukesh Patel's daughters were travelling in and had to crash-land near a village on the outskirts of Nashik. A small fire broke out in the aircraft. Dad immediately smashed the window pane with his walking stick and got Mukesh *bhai*'s daughters to climb out of the window to safety. He then tried to force open the little aircraft's jammed door with his shoulder and walking stick. Luckily there were some villagers nearby who managed to finally prise open the door. In typical fashion, Dad later said, "I wasn't bothered about my safety, but I could never forgive myself if anything had happened to Mukesh *bhai*'s daughters."

By the time he got the Patel family out of the plane, Dad's hair had been singed and he had a broken shoulder and foot. The pilot was very badly injured and lost his eyesight in the accident. The others escaped with a few broken bones. The villagers took them all to a hospital in Nashik, an hour's drive away. To Dad and his friends it felt like the longest hour they had ever known. From the hospital, Dad managed to call Priya, who was anxiously waiting for him at home. They were to attend a wedding that night and Priya was beside herself with worry. The moment she heard his voice, she demanded to know where Dad was and why he

was still out. In a matter-of-fact and calm tone, he explained: "Don't worry. I was in an accident. My plane crashed near Nashik and now I'm in hospital."

On hearing this, Priya's reaction was understandable: "I freaked out and panicked. I got into the car and drove to Nashik the same night. I reached the hospital and rushed in to see Dad. I was so relieved to see him safe and sound. We then arranged for everyone to be flown to Mumbai by helicopter. Dad was back in Breach Candy Hospital. The whole process of physiotherapy had to be started all over. It set him back a great deal, but within two months he was on his feet again. He was someone who refused to be beaten by adversity."

Dad's friend, Naresh Kotak, often visited him at Breach Candy and suggested he have treatment at the oldest *ayurvedic* centre in Kerala (which was located in Kottikal). He said the treatment might help strengthen Dad's limbs that had been weakened by the stroke. Uncle Naresh made all the necessary arrangements and personally accompanied Dad to Kottikal, where they spent a month. The *ayurvedic* treatment was a great help and Dad continued it on his return to Mumbai. Once again, Dad worked hard in the physiotherapy sessions because he didn't want to walk with a limp. Throughout his life, Dad could never show his wounds to the world. He soon went back to the Black Forest, accompanied by his friends and instead of their usual holiday, he had hydrotherapy treatment. His friends were so supportive and kept encouraging him. And it wasn't long before Dad was nearly a hundred per cent better.

The Last Days

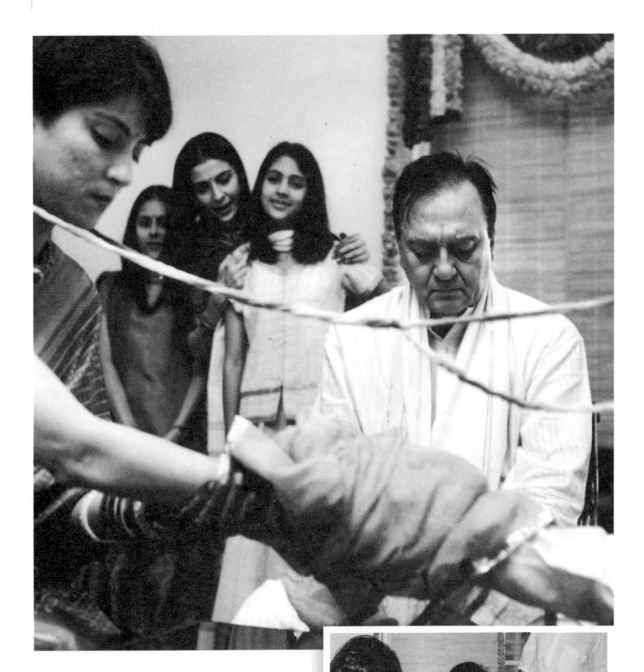

Dad had always wanted Sanjay to settle down and be happy. Despite all our hopes, Sanjay's marriage to Rhea Pillai broke up and amicably they parted ways. Sanjay's career, however, was doing better and better. The culmination of this upward swing was Rajkumar Hirani's wonderful film, *Munna Bhai MBBS* (2003), which ironically turned out to be Dad's last film and the only film in which father and son appeared together. Dad really enjoyed *Munna Bhai*. It gave him

an opportunity to stop worrying about Sanjay and revel instead in his success.

The whole experience was a great joy for Sanjay too: "Dad was so happy with my films and was especially proud of *Munna Bhai*. When Vinod Chopra came to him, he told me he refused, '*Maine pehle nahin bola* (I said no at first).' Then he thought to himself, '*Maine kaha yaar* acting is in the blood *to kar hi lo* (Acting is in the blood, I might as well do it).' The making of *Munna Bhai* was the happiest phase in his life. I have never seen Dad so happy and content. He used to tell me, '*Yaar, pata nahin main kahan politics mein aa gaya* (I don't know why I ever got into politics), this is my life.' He enjoyed the whole experience of being in front of the camera again. Maybe he felt a great sense of pride thinking, 'My son and I are acting together.'"

Another reason for celebration was Priya's marriage to Owen Roncon, whom she met while working at the Spastics Society. Owen runs an event management company and was organizing an event for the Spastics Society. Their decision to marry wasn't welcomed by Sanjay nor, more importantly,

Top: *(l to r)* Dad, Bunty, Namrata, Siya, Priya, Owen, Mrs Rajendra Kumar and Saachi.
Above: A few guests, including Dilip uncle and Saira aunty were invited for a surprise dinner to celebrate Priya and Owen's wedding.
Facing page: Priya and Owen Roncon had a simple and quiet wedding at home. Dad was hesitant to meet Owen but when he did, he approved of the marriage immediately. Sanjay was, however harder to convince. He did not attend the wedding and during the actual ceremony, he called Namrata continuously, telling her to stop the marriage. A year after the wedding, Sanjay visited Priya and Owen in their new home and reconciled with his new brother-in-law.
Preceding page 168: Priya was a shy and embarrassed bride and Dad and Namrata gently teased her.

Above: Priya's wedding to Owen was a moment of great joy for the whole family. Priya was always so close to Dad and being apart from him was inconceivable. But even after she got married, Owen and she would continue to see Dad almost every day.

Facing page (top): Relaxing with Dad at the Rocky Ranch are (*l to r*) Owen, Mohanty uncle and Bunty.

Facing page (bottom): The wonderful *Munna Bhai MBBS*, the only film in which Sanjay and Dad star together. This was Dad's last film.

by Dad. They were both worried as they felt Priya didn't know Owen that well and was making a mistake. Setting aside all misgivings, Dad finally said they should go ahead and get married if that's what Priya really wanted. Dad never believed in "dating," and initially refused to meet Owen. Dad was worried in case he didn't like him. Sanjay announced he'd have no contact with Owen for a year after the wedding. It was a difficult time for Priya, but she isn't the granddaughter of Jaddanbai, and daughter of Nargis for nothing!

A few days before the wedding, Dad gave in and met Owen. It was a happy meeting and in fact, during the last year of his life, he spent a lot of time with Owen and Bunty. Dad was content and relaxed now that Priya was getting married at last. We had a small ceremony at home in the presence of our immediate family members and a few friends. Dad wanted it that way and so did Priya. Without her knowing, Dad organized a dinner party on the terrace of Apsara. He invited his friends without

telling them why he had called them over. When they arrived, they were totally surprised to see Priya dressed as a bride and to meet Owen, Dad's second son-in law.

My mother's memory was as usual kept alive thanks to Dad. We continued to speak about her as though she was still around. All the ceremonies and *pujas* were held with a photograph of her placed in a prominent spot. During family weddings, her picture was right there next to Dad. When Priya got married, she was happy but felt sad as well: "After spending 37 years of my life with Dad, I was moving out of the house, leaving him alone. It broke my heart. So I continued to see him every day. I worked at the Spastics Society in Bandra till 2 P.M. and then would head to Dad's place and stay there till Owen picked me up in the evening. Namrata, Bunty, the children, Owen and me would meet at Dad's for lunch everyday. This was the ritual we had before I got married and, even to this day, the family

Top: Dad receiving in 1988 the Rajiv Gandhi National Sadbhavana Award for the promotion of peace and communal harmony from the late Dr Shankar Dayal Sharma, former President of India. Sonia Gandhi and former Prime Minister Narasimha Rao were also present.
Above: Dad visited Bhuj after the earthquake to help with relief work.
Facing page: Dad was appointed by Sonia Gandhi to lead the Sadbhavana movement in India to spread the message of peace and communal harmony, especially amongst young people. This movement gained popularity all over India through various peace marches and *yatras* (by jeep) in Kashmir, Gujarat and other states that were most affected.

continues to share a meal together every day."

In 2004, Dad's next elections were announced. We had never been actively involved in his political life – never campaigning or helping in any way and that's how he preferred it. This time round, Owen and Priya got involved in the planning of the election campaign. Owen had good organizational skills and great ideas, and Dad left it to him to design the campaign, which resulted in it being handled in a more professional manner. Dad's pamphlets were designed and interviews lined up. Dad really enjoyed this new and young approach. He won the elections – this was his fifth term as Member of Parliament.

Sonia Gandhi had always appreciated Dad's work and appointed him the President of the Sadhbhavana Ke Sipahi Movement in 2002 to spread peace and communal harmony in the country. This was something close to Dad's heart and he started work immediately. He got together a dedicated team. There were people from diverse professions and all walks of life. He set up groups in every city and appointed team leaders who would motivate the local youth and spread messages of peace and harmony. He organized peace marches in different parts of India, especially in Gujarat, which had suffered tremendously after the Godhra riots and in Kashmir as well. The movement grew in momentum, drawing in many young people. His success was well appreciated by the Party leadership. And to his surprise, in 2004, he was appointed the Union Minister for Youth Affairs and Sports in the newly formed government of the United Party Alliance. The credit can only go to Sonia Gandhi to have recognized his abilities and have chosen him. Despite all his sincerity, no one else had done this before. His appointment as Minister was an acknowledgment of his contribution to the Congress Party and the country.

As Dad said, "If it wasn't for Mrs Gandhi, I

would never have dreamt of becoming a Minister, nor did I work towards being one." The portfolio was well suited to Dad, although people laughingly said, "*Yeh kya ministry de di hai, isme to koi paise nahin hai* (What kind of Ministry has he been given? It has no funds whatsoever)." Affairs concerning the youth and sports were of paramount importance to Dad and he loved his new assignment. He was a sportsman himself – he loved trekking, was a great swimmer and horse rider. He used to parasail and took a keen interest in tennis and football. He believed the young were the future of India and wanted to do everything to help them.

In the last year of his life, Dad worked tirelessly. He was at his ministerial desk till midnight and would then return to his Delhi home where he'd carry on working. His was the only ministerial office to stay open that late. The next morning, he would start work early. If he called us in the middle of the night, I knew Dad had just stepped into his Delhi

Top: Dad in his ministerial office in Delhi with the family standing proudly behind him. He was Minister of Sports and Youth Affairs from 2004 to 2005.
Above: In Greece for the 2004 Olympics, Dad with tennis players Mahesh Bhupathi and Leander Paes.
Facing page: Sonia Gandhi requested Dad to organize the Dandi Yatra in Gujarat in 2005 to commemorate the anniversary of the historical Salt March of 1930.

home. He used to call us every day without fail. Even when he went on his *padayatras*, he'd make sure to call from a Circuit House en route. Dad was lonely in Delhi without us. He couldn't stay away from his family for too long. He had a few friends there, including Rajpal Singh Choudhury, Balbir Kakkad and his family, Mr Sagar Suri and Shakeel Ahmed. Shakeel Ahmed worked closely with Dad and became a confidante.

Dad had inadvertently created enemies and some people around him were filled with envy. He was shocked to discover these "so-called" friends were indeed people close to him and it hurt him deeply. He was a man who harmed no one, wishing only success for people who worked with him or for him. He went out of his way to help people and, as a result, many achieved great heights in their respective fields. Their progress and growth made him so proud. He never had an envious streak in him. When his own people went against him, it broke his spirit.

Once Dad got involved in the job, disillusionment set in. He was used to being his own boss and soon discovered all decision-making in most ministries was bound up in red tape. In one of our last conversations, he told me, "I'm tired. I can't do what I want to do. I can do nothing about the things happening under my very nose. I'm overstraining myself and my life doesn't seem to be in my control any more." He didn't say what was wrong, but just added, "Whatever I had hoped to do, I can't. The dreams I had of achieving things are getting destroyed."

My relationship with Dad was extremely close. I used to look after him like a mother. I became deeply attached to him emotionally and hated to see any bad press about him. I couldn't bear to see him hurt or in any sort of pain. I was protective of him and was his loudest supporter. But I also knew him well and knew Dad was perfect for the portfolio he had been given. Sports are so neglected in this vast country of a billion people. I am convinced he could have made a difference in youth affairs and sports, despite all the obstacles,

had he more support, encouragement and time.

During his last election campaign in 2004, Owen had organized a radio interview and Priya and Owen accompanied Dad to the radio station. When they got to the studio, Priya was asked to pose the last question to Dad. During the interview, Dad kept repeating that he had done everything in his life that he had ever wanted. So at that point Priya asked, "Dad, now you've done everything, is there anything you still want to do or see?" He replied on air, "You know what – I want you to give me a grandchild." In a later conversation Dad told Priya he wanted a grandson in the family, adding, "Sanju has a daughter and Namrata has two daughters."

Priya knew how important having a grandson was for Dad: "Dad believed if we had a boy, he would make him a sportsman. When I found out I was pregnant, he wasn't in town. I called him and said, 'Dad, I have something to tell you.' He said, 'Priya, now what?' He used to say I was always the one to announce bad news. 'You're going to be a grandfather again.' There was silence. 'It's the best news you've ever given me,' was his reply. He was particular that I tell no one until three months of my pregnancy were over. He gave Owen strict

instructions not to let me travel and made a list of directives for me to follow."

Despite the happy news, work was getting him down. He loved the challenge, but felt underused. When Dad got frustrated, he would take on more activity. In 2005, Sonia Gandhi asked him to organize the *Dandi Yatra* in Gujarat to commemorate the anniversary of Gandhiji's famous Salt March of 1930. Even though Dad was physically tired, he made up his mind to go. It was a huge success and at the end of the march, just about a month before he died, he decided to relax for a few days at Rocky

Ranch, the farm he owned off the Ahmedabad highway. Dad loved the farm and would often say that he would like to retire there some day and become a farmer again. Rocky Ranch was his retreat and escape from the world. After the *Dandi* march, Bunty and Owen, and some of Dad's political friends drove from Mumbai, laden with food and drink for the exhausted *padayatri*.

Bunty remembers those days vividly: "Usually when we went to Rocky Ranch, he'd wake us up in the morning and make us walk round the 25 acres. The farm had 300 mango trees, some teak, coconut and banana trees. We both loved the farm and, over time, we made it grow and flourish. I love the outdoors; I'm not a city person so Dad and I were happy there. I got to spend so much quality time with him. After the *Dandi* march, the last meal I would ever have with him was at the farm."

In 1996, our Pali Hill bungalow was pulled down and a high-rise apartment was to be built in its place. During the time (which ended up being many years) the new high-rise was under construction, we all had to live separately. We moved to Juhu

Above: An evening at home. Dad loved his dogs, especially Prince.
Right: With Mom gone, Dad knew he had to be the world for us.
Facing page (top): Dad with all the Rocky Ranch farm workers. Priya, Saachi and her father, Kumar Gaurav, accompanied him on this visit.
Facing page (bottom): Dad enjoying the sunshine at Rocky Ranch.

while Dad and Priya lived in a flat on the eighth floor of a building (Apsara Apartments) just down the road from our old bungalow. After 12 long years, the high-rise called Imperial Heights was finally ready. Our individual flats were designed according to our wishes and each of us had our own space. Dad was really looking forward to being under the same roof again. He was terribly excited about his new home and had personally designed the place, choosing all the furniture. It was around 20 May 2005 when he asked Priya to come to Delhi to help him buy some furniture. He was away in Kanpur for a function and met up with Priya later that night. She remembers being shocked to see Dad so unwell: "Papa was quite ill when he got back from Kanpur. He had fever and I asked him to rest. The next morning he attended prayer meetings held for Rajiv Gandhi's 14th death anniversary on 21 May. Then we chose some furniture for his new

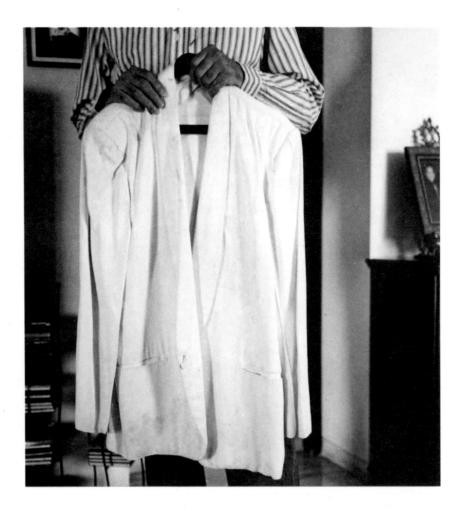

Right: 10 days before he passed away, he was packing to move into a new home at Imperial Heights, Bandra. Dad was a sentimental man and just as he had hung on to his old Fiat for years, he had carefully preserved the first jacket he could afford to buy and the one he wore as a radio presenter in the 1950s.

Facing page (top): This is the last family photograph. A few months later, Dad passed away. (*Back row, l to r*) Namrata, Bunty, Sanjay, Owen and Priya. Dad is flanked by Siya (*left*) and Saachi.

Facing page (bottom): When we were kids, Dad was a strict father. But as we grew up, we had our own ways of getting around him.

apartment. By the end of the day, he felt poorly and we took the next flight back to Mumbai."

Unusually for someone who was fastidious about his health, Dad refused to go to hospital. The doctor did various blood tests, and the reports were completely clear. Dr Puri watched over him, monitoring him closely. I spent the day with him on 23 May. He had a slight temperature, but was feeling better. He loved being pampered, especially when he was under the weather. I put a cold compress on his forehead and went to the kitchen to make him some tea and toast. While I was making the toast, Dad suddenly called for me. I said, "What is it now, Dad?" "You left a cold compress on my forehead, who will take it away? I'm not touching it. You put it on. You take it off!" It was moments like these when I would tell him how much I missed Mom. We

had a gentle banter and he seemed better. On 24 May there was a wedding in Bunty's family and it was a busy day for me. I kept calling Dad on his mobile to check on his health. I was upset when he didn't answer. He didn't have a landline in his room so I left messages with his staff, but he didn't call back. I couldn't go over to Dad's place that evening as I had to attend the wedding.

Owen and Priya had dinner with him on the night of 24 May. Priya remembers their conversation: "He had spent the entire day cleaning out his cupboard and packing his things in boxes to be carried to his new home. He chatted with Owen and me about the old days and gave Owen a photograph of me and Dad when I was a baby. He told Owen, 'It's for you.' Reminiscing about the past, he added, 'I have done everything in my life. I

have no regrets.' It was the last night I spent with him. I wanted to stay over but he said, 'I'll see you for tea in the morning.' He forced me to leave."

I called Priya from the wedding and she reassured me that Dad was feeling better and was ready to go to bed. Priya said he was tired as he had been busy packing all day and asked us both to come by the next morning. I should have insisted and gone that very night to see him. I will always regret my decision.

On the morning of 25 May, at around 10 A.M. the doorbell rang. It had a strange urgency. Priya entered screaming, saying something had happened to Dad. He had missed his nine o'clock appointment and wasn't waking up. We ran down the stairs of Imperial Heights when I realized no one had informed Sanjay. I rushed back Sanjay's 12th floor apartment and woke him out of his deep sleep.

Dad was still at the Apsara apartment down

the road. When I reached his flat on the eighth floor, I saw his staff was crying. I rushed into his room. Dad looked as though he was sleeping. His body was warm. We shook him to try and wake him, but he was gone. He must have passed away an hour or two before we all got there. Dad was 75.

We didn't get a chance to be alone with him on his final day. Once the news spread, people started pouring in. At one point, we locked the doors hoping to sit alone with him, but there were so many people in the house. To us he was Dad, but to the world he was a hugely popular figure. To this day, we wish we'd had a little more time with him. But we were in shock. It was all so sudden.

We were told later that Dad had woken up early in the morning when it was still dark. He came out of his room and Chottu, our cook, asked him if he wanted any tea. Dad said no and asked what time it was. Chottu said it must be around 5:30 or 6. Dad

exclaimed, "*Arre*, I am up too early. I'll go and take a nap. I have a nine o'clock appointment. I'll wake up in time." He went to the bathroom and changed into a fresh set of nightclothes. He brushed his teeth, had a wash and went back to bed. He must have slipped away from us around 8 A.M. The doctor said he had suffered a massive cardiac arrest – so he must have died instantly. Dad wasn't a heart patient, but even healthy people have heart attacks. Once the heart stops, there's nothing one can do. Many years earlier, he had to undergo an angioplasty, but this fatal episode didn't seem to have been triggered by anything in particular.

It was a crazy day. Sanjay was deeply distressed and could do nothing and sat there dazed. Bunty and Owen dressed Dad in a khadi *kurta pajama*, the kind of clothes he often wore. Sanjay couldn't bear seeing Dad. Even today, he can't bear to picture Dad lying on the bed, not breathing.

As the hours passed, the day became more and more chaotic. We didn't know what to do, but producer/director Vidhu Vinod Chopra, who had immediately come over to our place, took charge of the situation. I don't know how and why, but we looked to him for guidance as we would an elder brother. Vinod realized the state we were in and

Above (left): Prime Minister Manmohan Singh attended Dad's funeral and declared it a day of national mourning.
Above (right): Sonia Gandhi offering a prayer at Dad's *shraddhanjali*. This ceremony was held in Dad's ministerial bungalow in Delhi on the fourth day after his death.
Facing page: Wrapped in the tricolour, Dad's body is taken to the crematorium with hundreds of well-wishers, friends and family following his cortege, 25 May 2005.

handled everything, from talking to people to making all the arrangements. When we spoke to Vinod later, he too wondered how he had managed, never having faced a similar situation before. We got a call from Delhi saying Prime Minister Manmohan Singh and Sonia Gandhi wanted to attend the funeral and asked if we could postpone it for a day. The Prime Minister declared a state funeral for Dad and a national day of mourning.

We knew Dad would not have wanted his funeral to be delayed. He believed once something was over, it was over. We were in a state of utter shock. Yet the way events unfolded, it seemed as if a higher power was making things happen. We said we couldn't delay the funeral, as Dad would have wanted to go at once. For Hindus, all rituals must be performed before sunset. Appreciating the situation, the Prime Minister and Sonia Gandhi arrived a few hours later and the funeral took place

on 25 May 2005. We brought Dad's body from his apartment in Apsara to the newly constructed building, which stands in place of our old bungalow. Dad was covered in the Indian flag. We knew he would have thought this the highest honour, to leave the world in the embrace of the flag of a country he had worshipped. Sonia Gandhi and the Prime Minister left early, but Rahul Gandhi stayed till the end and came with us to the cremation ground for the last rites.

We took Dad in an open truck to the crematorium at Santa Cruz. Thousands of people belonging to all classes, communities and castes came from everywhere to witness his final departure. Later we heard stories from acquaintances and strangers all over India about how

he always replied to their letters and demands. His answers always had a personal touch and were signed in his own hand. He never forgot a friend's birthday or anniversary. He touched the hearts of so many thousands and throughout his life remained a peoples' person. And they showed him their love and respect by walking with him on his last journey.

There was a 21-gun salute for Dad. Many political colleagues and adversaries were present while the cremation and the last rites were performed. Dad was Superman to us and the idea that he was invincible was deeply etched in our minds. Now suddenly we had to face this terrible day and could hardly absorb the depressing reality of his death. He was Mom and Dad in one soul. Now we had lost Dad and Mom once again.

The eldest son is required to collect the ashes, but the next morning, Owen, Priya and Bunty went instead of Sanjay because he was so overcome with grief. He just couldn't handle going to the cremation ground. But we had to somehow do what was needed. When Priya and Bunty went to collect the ashes, she was told a woman wasn't allowed to enter the cremation ground or collect the ashes. But Priya was adamant: "I was four months pregnant then. I went against convention because I wanted to be with my father till the end. I wanted to be there at every stage, to see the pyre burn, collect his ashes and bones from the pyre and immerse them. It gave me a sense of acceptance, closure, and an understanding of life and beyond."

Dad had once told Priya, "When I'm no more I want to be immersed in the Ganges where it is the purest." Remembering his words, Priya said that we must do what Dad had wished. We were told we couldn't go to Gangotri, so the next best place was Rishikesh. Viveik Oberoi knew of an *ashram* (Parmarth Niketan) and said he'd make all the arrangements. Once again, it felt as though a higher power was guiding us. We took Dad's ashes to Delhi and from there, we went to our grandmother's *samadhi* in Mandoli, in Haryana, because whenever Dad began anything new, he'd go there first. From Mandoli, we made our way to the final destination.

Above: As we performed the last rites for Dad in Rishikesh, it started to dawn on us that he was no more. Our stunned expressions say it all.
Facing page: Owen, Priya and Bunty went the next day to collect Dad's ashes at the crematorium.

I think we probably don't need to go on any spiritual *yatra* ever again, because we experienced so much on Dad's last journey. As we neared the border of each district, we saw hundreds of people on the road, waiting for us. They had heard we were taking Dad's ashes to Rishikesh and had stood for hours with flowers in their hands to shower on the passing car. We had never quite realized how many hearts Dad had touched. This was the kind of respect usually reserved for saints and holy men and women. People were showing Dad the same kind of respect. The six-hour journey to Rishikesh in fact took us 10 hours. We reached the *ashram*, Parmarth

Niketan, in the evening. The atmosphere was electric. Swamiji Chidananda Saraswati performed the evening *aarti* on the banks of the Ganges. The whole place glowed bright with the light of *diyas*. There was a magical, heavenly feeling in the air.

I think the most difficult moment for us was the next day when we had to immerse Dad's ashes and finally let go. Then we understood the meaning of these rituals. Dad used to tell us how rites and rituals prepare one for finality. Everything we did on that journey, until the moment of immersion, brought us closer and closer to accepting the loss of a loved one and the finality of death. Everything that happened during the journey, culminating at the Swami Samarth *ashram* in Rishikesh, seemed to have the touch of the divine. We were happy because we knew that Dad would have wanted it this way.

Left: Dad's friends, Jaywant and Rajni Ulhal (accompanied by Joginder Singh and Mohanty uncle) return to the Black Forest where many wonderful days were spent with Dad to scatter some of his ashes at the places he loved to visit.

Below: We planted two trees in memory of Mom and Dad at our farm Rocky Ranch and mixed his ashes with the soil that covered the plants.

Facing page (top and bottom): The rituals over. Each of us say our last farewell.

The Legacy

Life without Mom and Dad was difficult for us to ever imagine. Now it is something we have to face every day. They gave us so much love, understanding and values and in many ways we feel they are still with us. Every time we have a problem, we ask ourselves, "How would Dad handle it? What would Mom do?" They were such real people. They faced countless difficulties and yet managed to smile through their ordeals. Despite their enormous strength, Mom and Dad were deeply sentimental. Sometimes it feels as though Dad, in particular, collected family memorabilia, preserved so many documents, and dated countless photographs, so that one day we might revisit the past. This foresight is at the heart of this book but their greatest legacy is the memory of the kind of people they were. Through that we try to shape our lives and try to live up to the standards they set.

In the new high-rise building Imperial Heights, which now stands on the site of our old bungalow, Dad made apartments for each of us so we would never be lonely. In early 2005, Priya first moved in; Bunty, our daughters and I followed at the beginning of March of the same year. And finally Sanjay joined us. We had always hoped that Dad would live in his penthouse and move in as he had planned on his birthday on 6 June. But it was not meant to be.

Sanjay looks back on the past years: "There was a time when we were living separately. Namrata and Bunty were in Juhu, Dad was with Priya in Apsara Apartments. I was married for the second time and had moved out too. The family had broken up. But before Dad passed away, he planned the most amazing thing – that we'd all be together again. We may live in separate flats, but we're in the same building. Priya and Owen, Anju, Bunts and their children, we're together again. We still share a meal every day. And this is how he planned it. If he had passed away in Imperial Heights, I guarantee none of us would have been happy living here. I wouldn't have stayed here. None of us would have."

We feel Dad has "moved" in with us. We sense his presence everywhere, especially in his own apartment, which is exactly as he would have wanted it. I have arranged his clothes, books and personal papers meticulously. We even had a *griha pravesh* ceremony performed in Mom and Dad's new home. We share family meals in their dining room and in their kitchen, food is cooked for us. It remains the home of our parents, and we know they are with us all the time.

Mom and Dad live on in other ways too. Not only in us siblings, but in their grandchildren too. Priya's greatest consolation is the fact that Dad knew about her pregnancy: "Dad passed away knowing I was pregnant and knowing another grandchild was on the way. The months following his death were tough for me, but I faced them believing that Dad was protecting me and my baby. When I look back, I wonder how I managed to do anything at all and can only think he was helping me. Dad had never seen a sonogram and I had so wanted him to come with me when I was going to have it done, so he would see the image of the baby. Ironically, I had an appointment for a sonogram two days after he died. I'm so glad he knew I was expecting, despite the fact he will never know now he has the grandson he so wanted. When Mom died, Dad kept her memory alive. We always spoke of her, as if she was still around, and now we think of Dad in the same way. I feel his presence in everything I do. I want to keep their memories alive for my son Siddharth. He must learn about his grandparents. Out of the blue, he will suddenly say 'Nana' and 'Nani' and point to photographs of them."

Dad loved my two girls, Saachi and Siya. Siya and he had a special bond. He would call her every

Facing page: The *griha pravesh* ceremony at our parents' new apartment was a solemn affair. As ever, Yusuf uncle and Saira aunty were there for us, seeing us through the good times and the bad.
Preceding page 188: The *griha pravesh* ceremony took place a month after Dad passed away in what was to be his apartment in Imperial Heights. This highrise now stands on the site of our old Pali Hill bungalow and the road on which it is located has since been renamed Nargis Dutt Road.

day, no matter where he was in the world. He used to call her "Siyaji." When I first gave her a mobile phone, he didn't like the idea at all, but later said it was the best thing I had ever done. Now he could call her directly. He used to talk to her about everything; telling her how his day had been and asking her what kind of day she had. This was their daily routine. He once called at 11:30 at night and said, "*Siyaji se baat karni thi, par phone band hai* (I wanted to speak to Siyaji but her mobile is switched off)." I explained she was sleeping and had school the next day. That's when he realized he had called very late at night.

Dad had a beautiful relationship with all his granddaughters including Trishala. Although she lives in New York, he made it a point to keep in touch with her. Dad had chosen the names for all his grandchildren – Trishala, Saachi, Siya. When Priya's son, Siddharth, whom Dad never saw, uttered his first word, he said "Nana" (Grandpa). The little boy recognizes Dad when he sees his photograph, as if a strong previous-life connected them.

We miss Mom and Dad every minute of the day. No matter how old you are, there will always be a void. There are so many things we long to share with them. And the most important of all was the court verdict concerning Sanjay. Thirteen long years since Sanjay's arrest on his return from Mauritius in 1993, his judgment was announced on 28 November 2006. It was a hugely tense day and we didn't know what to expect. Either Sanjay would come home with us or be incarcerated immediately. He was uneasy and kept silent. We dropped him outside the courtroom and waited in a nearby hotel. Some hours passed and finally the news came. Sanjay had been convicted under the Arms Act, but TADA did not apply to him and the judge clearly

Dad doted on his grandchildren and they doted on him in equal measure.

Left: We knew that Dad always wanted a grandson. Owen, Priya and their first born, Siddharth, on holiday. Priya was pleased that at least Dad knew a grandson was on the way.

Above: Our parents have instilled the importance of family in us. We try and communicate the same ideas to our own children. So Mr and Mrs Dutt will live on in them as they will always live in us.

Facing page: They had both acted in many movies as lead heroes, but Dad and Sanjay only shared screen space in one film, *Munna Bhai MBBS*. Despite all the brilliant humour in this film, at the heart of the story is a son's desire to win his father's approval. This was true of Dad and Sanjay's personal relationship as well.

stated that Sanjay Dutt is not a terrorist. When Priya and I heard the news, we knew this was the only thing that Dad had wanted to hear – that his son was not an anti-national. We were deeply sad to think Dad had left this world without knowing what we now know. Whatever happens to Sanjay, we believe Mom and Dad have given us the strength to face up to it. We imagine that they are still watching over us somewhere. At times, even this is little consolation. If only we could turn back the clock to the time before we lost Mom and Dad forever.

Sanjay will never forget a dream he once had: "Three days after Dad passed away, he came to me in a dream. That dream is so clear in my head, even today. We are in the old bungalow. My car drives in and Dad is standing on the steps. I go to him and ask, 'Where did you go? Why did you leave us?' He just hugs me and takes me inside the house. He says, 'Son, now that I'm not here, you are the eldest in the family. You have to take care of your sisters and everybody.' I start crying and ask, 'Why are you saying all this? Come back and stay here with us.' He answers, 'No, I'm happy.' And he gives me a lot of love and then says, 'I have to go now.' We are upstairs in his bedroom and I say, 'Please don't go, don't go and leave us again.' Then suddenly I wake up."

Above: On the walls of our new homes at Imperial Heights hang pictures of our parents. When friends and family enter the room they often comment that Mom and Dad's presence feels tangible.
Facing page: When Dad was reading a book, he would often jot down inspiring quotes in a journal.

HE WHO REGARDS
WELL-WISHERS
FRIENDS — FOES
NEUTRALS — MEDIATORS
THE OBJECTS OF HATRED
RELATIVES
THE VIRTUOUS AND THE
SINFUL-ALIKE,
STANDS SUPREME

RIGVEDA. VI-9.

YOU CANNOT
DISCOVER
NEW — OCEANS
UNLESS YOU HAVE
THE COURAGE
TO LOSE SIGHT
OF THE
SHORE.

Over the years, one learns the art of living, of forgiving, but by then it is too late.
Your body gives way. All one can hope is your children will learn from your experiences
and make a better future than your present. And even if they don't, it doesn't matter.
Nothing matters as long as you can spread happiness and live in peace.

Sunil Dutt, March 1991

ISBN: 978-81-7436-455-5

© **Namrata Dutt Kumar & Priya Dutt, 2007**
Second impression

Published in India by
Roli Books Pvt. Ltd.
M-75, Greater Kailash-II Market
New Delhi 110 048, India.
Phone: ++91-11-29212271, 29212782
Fax: ++91-11-29217185
Email: roli@vsnl.com
Website: rolibooks.com

Editors: Nasreen Munni Kabir, Priyanka Chowdhury & Priya Kapoor
Design: Mukesh Singh
Production: Kumar Raman & Naresh Nigam

Printed and bound at Gopsons Papers Ltd., Noida.